Medieval Realms

Britain 1066–1500

Neil Tonge and
Peter Hepplewhite

Stanley Thornes (Publishers) Ltd

Designed and typeset by Hilary Norman
Artwork by Peter Harper and Beverly Curl
Cover artwork by Lee Montgomery, Beehive Illustration
Picture research by Julia Hanson

First published in 1997 by:
Stanley Thornes (Publishers) Ltd
Ellenborough House
Wellington Street
CHELTENHAM GL50 1YW
England

97 98 99 00 / 10 9 8 7 6 5 4 3 2 1

A catalogue record for this book is available from the British Library.

ISBN 0-7487-2425-7

Printed in Hong Kong

Acknowledgements

The authors and publishers are grateful to the following for permission to reproduce illustrations and photographs in this book.

Ancient Art and Architecture Collection 80;
Bibliothèque Nationale, Paris 721;
Bodleian Library, Oxford 491 (Ms Laud Misc. 720 f. 226v), 74r (MS Ashmole 391 (v) f. 10 r), 78 (MS Douce 313);
Bridgeman Art Library 30t (Signing of the Magna Carta by Charles Sims/Houses of Parliament, London), 34 (Add. 18855 f. 108 British Library, London), 36t (Westminster Abbey, London), 431 (Cott Claud DVI f. 12v British Library), 52t (Arundel 38 f.37 British Library), 54b (Add. 24189 f. 8 British Library), 56 (Fr 4276 f. 6 Bibliothèque Nationale, Paris), 58 (Fr 20124 f. 331 Bibliothèque Nationale, Paris), 72tr (St. Francis Preaching to the Birds by Giotto, San Francesco/Upper Church, Assisi), 75tl (Roy 15 E II f. 165 British Library), 75br (Harl 1585 f. 97v British Library), 76 (BL Add. 19720 f. 165820), 81 (Private Collection), 82 (Add. 27695 f.14 British Library), 85bl (The Wilton Diptych/National Gallery, London), 87r (Fr 12420 f. 86 Bibliothèque Nationale, Paris); Bristol Record Office 64;
British Library 7tl (Royal 14EI. f. 3), tc (Add. 1712 f. 6) & tr (Royal 2 BVII f. 78v), 191, 26b (Add. Ch. 5719 Obv.), 27 (Cott. Claud BII f. 341), 28 (Har. 5102 f. 32), 32t (Claud B IV f. 59), 35, 37 (Roy 18.E.1 f.165v.), 38 (Roy. 20.C. vii f.133), 52b (Roy. 20. c.VII f. 41v), 60t (Add. 42130 f. 172), 62 (Add. 42130 f. 170), 66 (Roy 15 E.11 f. 265), 70 (SL 2435 f. 44v), 711 (Cott. Dom-A XVII f. 122v), 76 (Add. 19720 f. 165), 85br, 871 (Add. 24189 f. 16), 88t (Roy 19.B.XV. f. 37), 88b (Add. 42130 f. 39r);
British Museum, London 7cr;
Cambridge University Collection of Air Photographs/(c) Crown Copyright/MOD. Reproduced with the Permission of the Controller of HMSO 59t;
Corpus Christi College 24 (all);
By permission of the Dean and Chapter, Durham Cathedral 93b;
Durham County Council 93t;
ET Archive 67b, 68b;
Mary Evans Picture Library 42, 48, 69t;
Sonia Halliday 25t, 65t;
Michael Holford 81, 9t & C, 12t, 13t & b, 14r, 16bl, 17, 22, 25b, 69b;
A.F. Kersting 85tr;
Kobal Collection 30b, 72br;
Mansell Collection 55b, 74b, 891;
Mas 86;
Royal Collection (c) HM The Queen 32b;
Peter Smith Photography, Malton 92;
Spectrum Colour Library 60b, 67t;
Universitatsbibliothek, Heidelberg 91 (Cod. Pal. Germ. 848 f. 82v);
Visual Arts Library 75tr, 89r, 90 (both).

Every effort has been made to contact copyright holders and we apologise if any have been overlooked.

Contents

Transformations

What changes took place in medieval times?

What does 'medieval' mean?

The medieval period is what **historians** call the time from the Norman Conquest of England in 1066 to when Henry Tudor became King in 1485. Another name for this period of history is the 'Middle Ages'. Medieval comes from the Latin language and also means 'middle'. It is called the 'Middle Ages' because it came between the ancient time of the Romans and modern times.

How much did things change in the medieval period?

This book will take you on a journey through four hundred years. You will need to keep a record of that journey and so, as you go, make a note of those things that changed a lot, and things that changed very little.

Changes in the landscape

Here are two illustrations of Newcastle upon Tyne, in the north-east of England. The first one shows the town as it would have looked in 1080, when a Norman castle was built. The second illustration shows the town in about 1500. What changes can you see?

Remember, this tells us only about changes in one town. Do you know what changes took place in your town? What happened to the rest of the country? Historians look for many different kinds of evidence, to try and build up a more complete picture of the Middle Ages – like putting together pieces of a jigsaw.

A wooden **motte** and **bailey** castle is built by Robert Curthose to control the surrounding area. It is built on the ruins of a Roman fort

Source A
Newcastle in 1080

More trade in the surrounding countryside. Many local people come to sell their goods at the markets in the town

The Roman bridge is replaced by another stone bridge, with houses built on it

Source B Newcastle in 1500

Historians People who study history.
Mud and wattle Twigs woven together and then covered in mud, to make walls.
Motte and bailey castle A wooden tower built on a hill, with a courtyard around it.
Cathedral A large church.

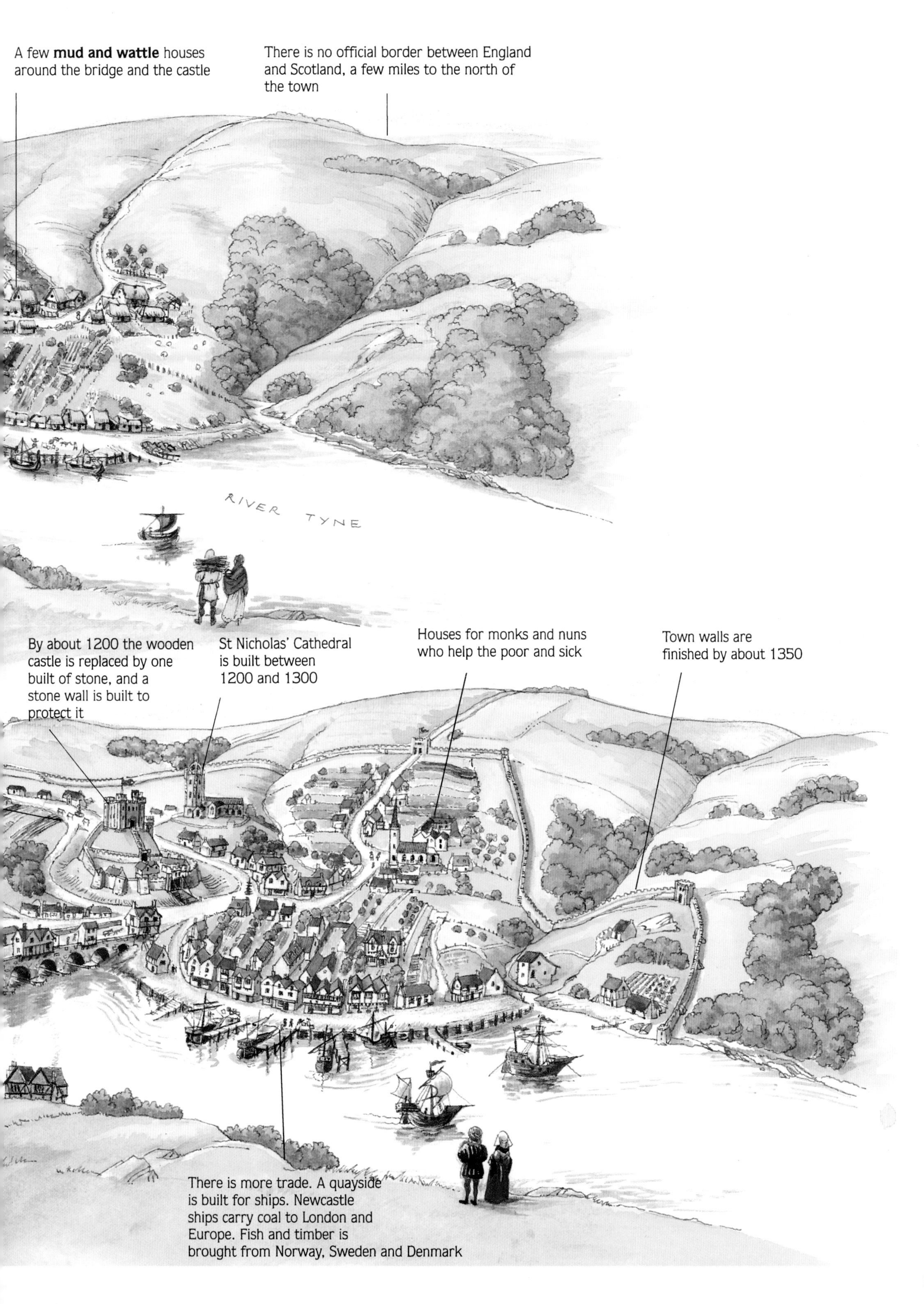
A few **mud and wattle** houses around the bridge and the castle
There is no official border between England and Scotland, a few miles to the north of the town
RIVER TYNE
By about 1200 the wooden castle is replaced by one built of stone, and a stone wall is built to protect it
St Nicholas' Cathedral is built between 1200 and 1300
Houses for monks and nuns who help the poor and sick
Town walls are finished by about 1350
There is more trade. A quayside is built for ships. Newcastle ships carry coal to London and Europe. Fish and timber is brought from Norway, Sweden and Denmark

1 The Normans
Claiming a kingdom

Why was there a crisis in England in 1066?

Why is 1066 the most famous date in English history?

How would you feel if Britain was invaded today? Imagine an enemy tank on your street corner and a foreign flag flying over your school. The last successful invasion of England happened in 1066 when the Normans won the Battle of Hastings. This changed the course of British history.

English nobles were driven out and their land given to Norman **barons**. Castles were built to control the countryside. By 1200 almost every English cathedral and abbey had been demolished. They were replaced by bigger and grander Norman buildings. The new rulers spoke French, and English became a second-class language. Up to this time, Viking settlers had given England close links to Scandinavia. After the Norman **Conquest** England was tied to Normandy and France.

Source B A monk, William of Malmesbury, writing in 1120 about the Battle of Hastings

> This was a fatal day for England, a sad wrecking of our dear country caused by the **domination** of new lords.

Source C

The history of the English people up to 1066	
400 BC	Celtic tribes from Europe settle in Britain
AD 43	Roman conquest of Britain begins. Some Romans settle in Britain and stay.
AD 410	Roman army withdraws from Britain, leaving the Celts to defend themselves.
AD 450	Angles, Saxons and Jutes come from Europe and begin to settle. Celts loose control of much of Britain.
AD 793	First recorded Viking raid from Scandinavia. Over the next hundred years the Vikings take over most of northern and eastern England.

Source A The last time Britain came close to being invaded was during the Second World War. If German troops had invaded, this is what we might have seen.

A rich prize: England in 1066

In 1066 England was a rich and well-ordered country with a population of 1.5 million people. English towns were called Burhs. They were centres of trade and often had walls for protection. Only about 20 towns had a population of more than a thousand. Most people lived in the countryside. They were peasants, or serfs, who worked on the land of the local lord, or **thegn**.

Source D The life of a peasant. Written by Aelfric, a monk, in about AD 1000

> I work hard. I go out at daybreak, drive the oxen to the field and yoke them to the plough. Even in a hard winter I dare not stay at home because I am afraid of my lord. Every day I must plough a full acre or more. Mighty hard work it is, for I am not free.

Key words

Baron Norman nobleman.
Conquest Attacking a country and taking over the people by force.
Domination Control.
Thegn English nobleman.

Source E England's wealth in 1066

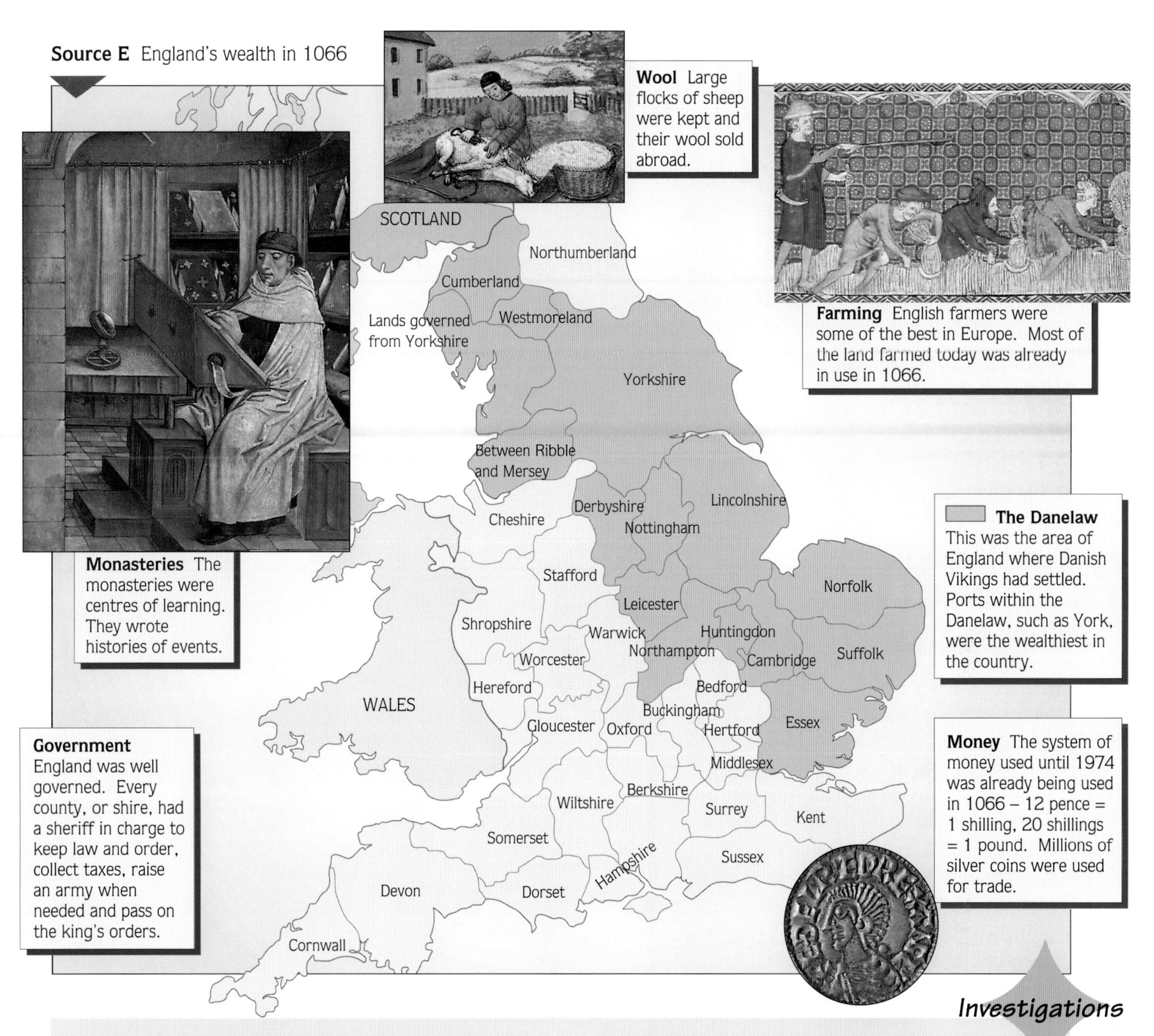

Investigations

1 Look at Source **A**. If you were planning an invasion of England now, what places would you try to capture or destroy first? Make a list.

2 Copy this table, and use the information on page 6 to complete it.

Results of the Norman Conquest (in order of importance)

Result	Reasons for my choice
1	
2	
3	
4	
5	

3 The people of England in 1066 are often called Anglo-Saxons. Use Source **C** to explain whether you think this is an accurate description of them.

4 What does Source **D** tell us about how England's wealth was shared out in 1066?

5 Look at the map in Source **E**. Which shire do you live in? Was it ruled by the English or the Danelaw in 1066? Does it have the same name now?

6 After 1066 some Norman writers claimed that England was a backward country. Looking at Source **E**, do you agree with them? Explain your answer.

Remember...

- **The Norman Conquest changed the course of British history**
- **England was a rich, well organised country in 1066.**

Three rivals for the throne of England

- **Who claimed the English throne after the death of Edward the Confessor?**
- **What were their claims?**

In January 1066 the King of England, Edward the Confessor, died. He had no son to follow him as king. Three people thought they should rule England. To understand each of their claims to be king, we must piece together the surviving evidence.

Source A How England was divided between the earls in 1065

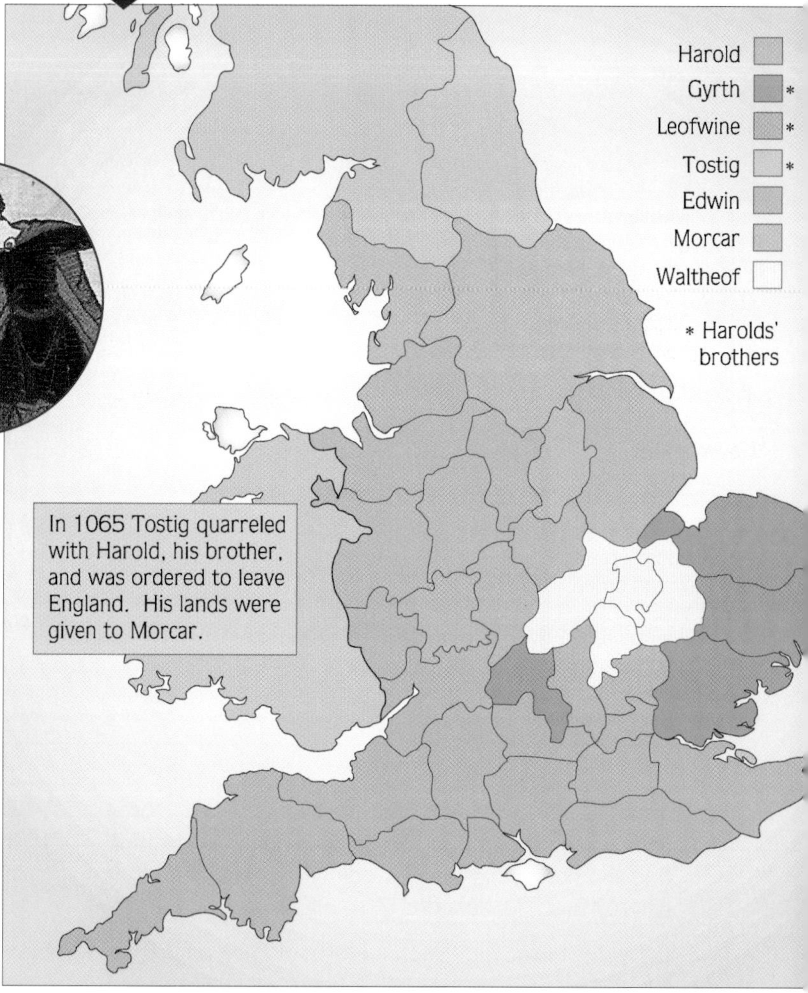

Harold
Gyrth *
Leofwine *
Tostig *
Edwin
Morcar
Waltheof

* Harolds' brothers

In 1065 Tostig quarreled with Harold, his brother, and was ordered to leave England. His lands were given to Morcar.

Harold Godwinson's claim

Harold Godwinson

Position in 1066: **Earl** of Wessex – the most powerful nobleman in England.

Family History: His father, Earl Godwin, built up the family fortunes during the reign of King Canute. In 1051 he rebelled against King Edward and forced him to get rid of friends and advisers from Normandy.

Connections with King Edward: Harold's sister Edith married Edward.

Achievements: Harold served Edward better than his father had. He almost ran the kingdom for him, without trying to take over. A good warrior, he defeated the Welsh King Gruffyd in 1063.

Source B King Edward's promise to Harold, 5 January 1066. From the *Anglo-Saxon* ***Chronicle***, written by English monks

On his deathbed that wise king [Edward] had promised the kingdom to Harold, a great noble. This was because Harold had always been loyal: he had carried out all the king's commands.

Source C The coronation of Harold, described by an English monk, Florence of Worcester, writing in about 1115

Harold, son of Earl Godwin, was chosen king by the chief noblemen of England. On the same day [6 January] Harold was crowned by Aldred, Archbishop of York, with great ceremony.

Key words

Chronicle A record of events, often written by monks.
Earl Powerful noble.

Duke William of Normandy's claim

Duke William of Normandy

Position in 1066: Ruler of Normandy, the strongest part of France.

Family History: Normandy was a Viking kingdom established in France by William's ancestor, Rollo, in 911. William was the son of Robert I. He became Duke in 1035, when he was still a boy. Most of his life was spent fighting to defend his lands.

His enemies nicknamed him William the Bastard because he was illegitimate – his father was not married to his mother.

Connections with King Edward: Edward lived in Normandy from 1016 to 1042, after the Danish King Canute took the throne from Edward's father, King Aethelred. Edward's mother Emma was William's aunt. Edward promised the throne of England to William in 1051 after William sent troops to England to help him fight Earl Godwinson.

Achievements: William was a skilled and ruthless soldier. In 1054 and 1057 he defeated invading armies sent by the King of France.

Source D This section of the Bayeux Tapestry shows the events of 1064. Harold swears to be loyal to William. He swears his oath on a casket containing holy **relics**.

The Bayeux Tapestry

The Bayeux Tapestry is one of our main sources of information on the events of 1066. It is 70 metres long and 20 inches wide. It was embroidered in Kent in about 1070, probably on the instructions of Bishop Odo, William's brother.

Source E Written by William of Poitiers, priest to the family of Duke William, in about 1070

> King Edward, who loved William like a brother, felt the hour of his death was near. He sent Harold to William to swear an oath that William would become king. Many truthful men who were there say that Harold swore of his own free will.
>
> Later came the news that this headstrong Englishman seized the throne with the help of his evil supporters. He was crowned by Stigand, who the **Pope** had ordered should no longer be a priest.

Relics Holy objects such as the bones of saints.
Pope Leader of the Catholic Church (see page 25). In the Middle Ages everyone in Western Europe was Catholic.

Investigations

In Source **D**, why does Harold swear his oath to William on a casket of holy relics?

Harald Hardrada's claim

Harald Hardrada

Position in 1066: King of Norway.

Family History: Harald was half-brother to King Olaf of Norway. In 1030, when he was only fifteen, he was forced to flee abroad when Olaf was killed in battle. Harald made his fortune serving as a soldier in Constantinople and returned to take the throne of Norway in 1045.

Connections with King Edward: None. Harald believed he had a right to the throne of England because King Canute had ruled Norway, Denmark and England from 1016 to 1035.

Achievements: Harald had a fearsome reputation as a warrior, but had wasted many years fighting wars for the throne of Denmark.

Source F Tostig, Harold Godwinson's brother, joins Harald. From the *Anglo-Saxon Chronicle*.

In September 1066 Earl Tostig sailed into the Humber with 60 ships and was driven away by Earl Edwin. He sailed to Scotland with 12 small ships and there Harald, King of Norway met him with 300 ships and Tostig submitted to him and promised to serve him.

Remember...

- **Harold Godwinson became King of England in January 1066.**
- **Duke William of Normandy claimed that the throne of England had been promised to him.**
- **Harald Hardrada, King of Norway, also claimed the throne of England.**

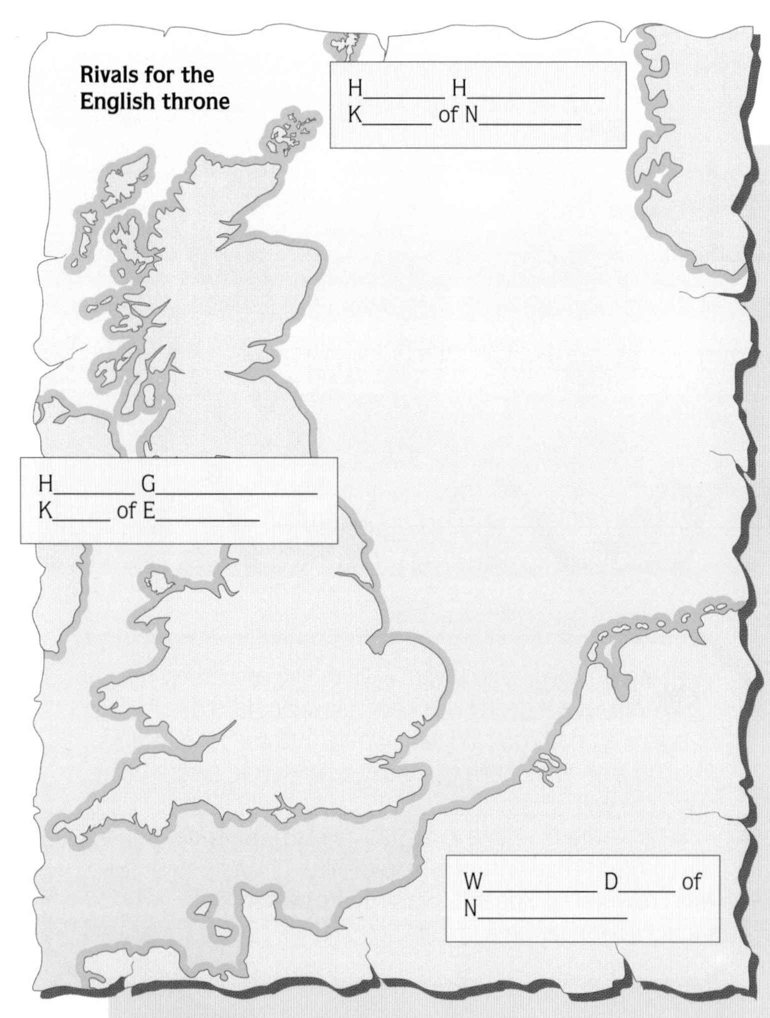

1 Copy out the map above. Finish the names and choose 3 colours to shade in the kingdoms.

Investigations

2 Compare the biography box on this page with those on pages 8 and 9. Who was the closest relative of King Edward?

3 What does Source **A** on page 8 tell us about Harold Godwinson and his brothers in 1065? How would this help Harold?

4 Look again at Source **A** on page 8. Who was Tostig? Would the events in Source **F** make Harald Hardrada's claim to the throne stronger or weaker?

5 Who had the strongest claim to the throne of England? Harold Godwinson, William of Normandy or Harald Hardrada? Copy out the following table and use Sources **B–F** to help you fill it in.

Who had the strongest claim?

	Strengths	Weaknesses
Harold Godwinson		
William of Normandy		
Harald Hardrada		

Winning a kingdom

How did William become King of England?

The Battle of Stamford Bridge

King Harold knew he would have a hard fight to hold onto England. He did not know which of his enemies would make the first move, where they would attack, or when. Harold gambled that William would attack first.

Throughout the summer of 1066 Harold's army stood ready on the south coast, while his ships patrolled the Channel. But William's army did not come. In mid-September Harold ordered his forces to go home. A few days later, he received an urgent message. Harald Hardrada had landed near York.

Source A Harold moves against Hardrada

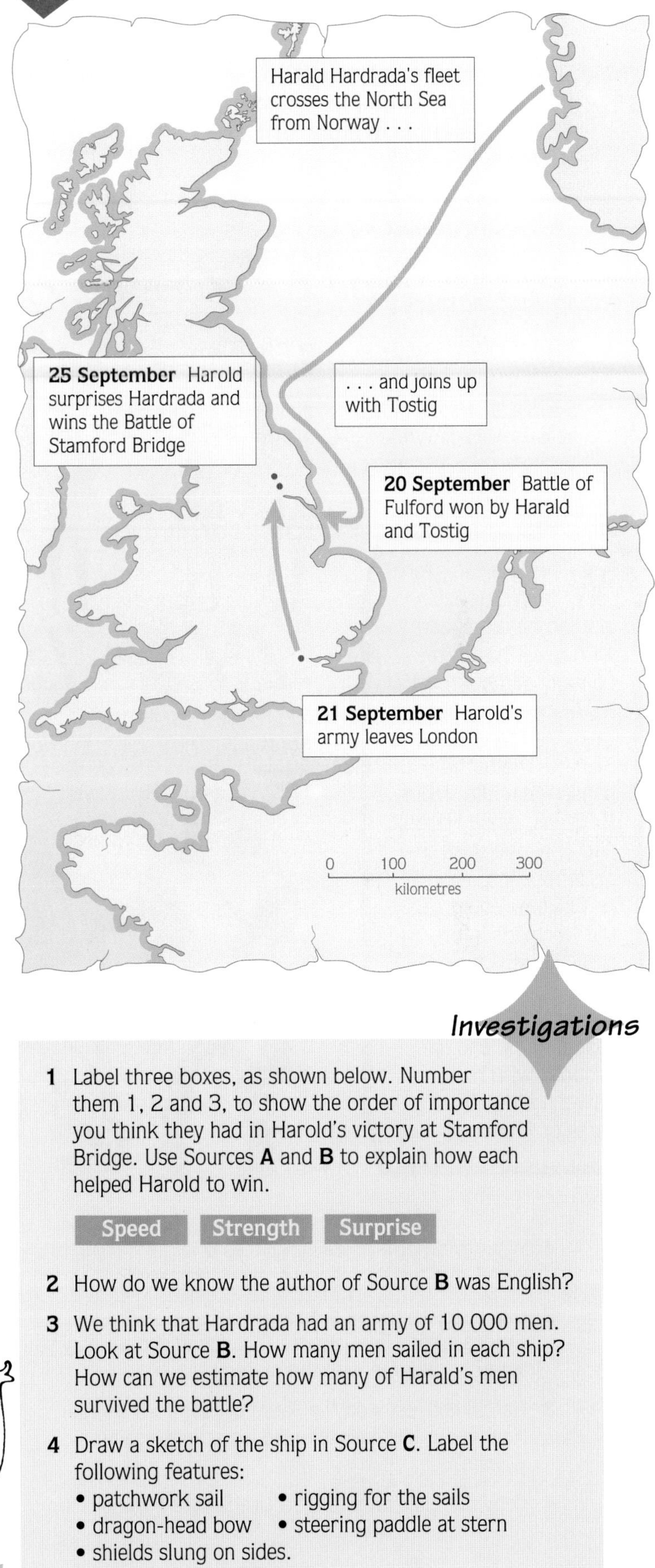

Source B Harold wins the Battle of Stamford Bridge. From the *Anglo-Saxon Chronicle*.

Harald King of Norway and Tostig sailed with 300 ships into the Humber until they came to York. Earls Edwin and Morcar fought them [at the Battle of Fulford] but the **Northmen** won. Then Harold our king surprised and attacked them at Stamford Bridge with a great force of Englishmen. All day a fierce battle raged. Hardrada and Tostig were killed and the Northmen fled. The English chased them until they reached their ships, and some were drowned and some were burnt. Only 24 ships returned to Norway.

Source C Hardrada's ships would have looked like this carving on a stone, found on the island of Gotland, near Sweden. This carving was done at about the same time that Harald Hardrada was alive.

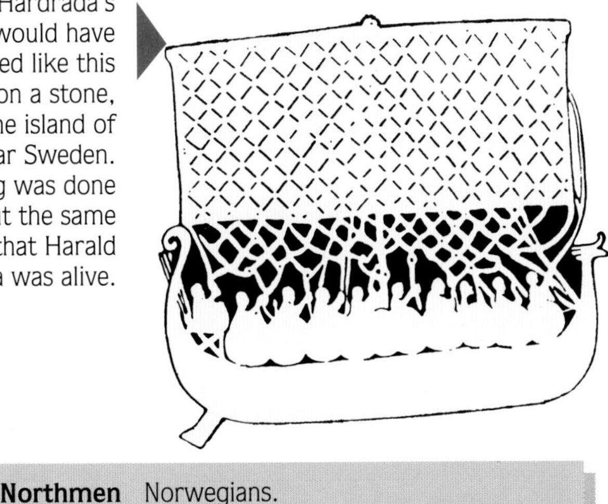

Key words

Northmen Norwegians.

Investigations

1 Label three boxes, as shown below. Number them 1, 2 and 3, to show the order of importance you think they had in Harold's victory at Stamford Bridge. Use Sources **A** and **B** to explain how each helped Harold to win.

Speed | Strength | Surprise

2 How do we know the author of Source **B** was English?

3 We think that Hardrada had an army of 10 000 men. Look at Source **B**. How many men sailed in each ship? How can we estimate how many of Harald's men survived the battle?

4 Draw a sketch of the ship in Source **C**. Label the following features:
- patchwork sail
- rigging for the sails
- dragon-head bow
- steering paddle at stern
- shields slung on sides.

What are the crew doing?

The Normans land in Sussex

Harold had won a brilliant victory. He had destroyed two of his enemies, but he had little time to enjoy his success. Events began to move very quickly.

Countdown to the Battle of Hastings

- **28 September** William's army lands near Pevensey in Sussex.
- **2 October** News reaches Harold in York. He sets out for London straight away.
- **6–11 October** Harold reaches London and gathers another army.
- **11–13 October** Harold and his army march south and set up camp on Senlac Hill, near Hastings.

Source D The Bayeux Tapestry, showing the Normans loading supplies for the invasion of England

Source E Harold moves against William. Written by Florence of Worcester in about 1115.

When Harold heard of William's landing he marched with great haste to London. Although half his troops were not yet ready he marched on to Sussex. The battle began nine miles from Hastings, when Harold had only one third of his troops in position.

William, Count of the Normans had arrived with countless hosts of horsemen, slingers, and footsoldiers, and had brought with him powerful help from all parts of France.

Source F The English and Norman armies

Investigations

1. What evidence is there in Sources **D** and **E** that the Normans were well prepared?
2. One historian has said that 'Harold's haste was a serious error'. Read Source **E** and then explain why you agree or disagree with this statement.
3. Harold had just won the Battle of Stamford Bridge. How might this have affected his actions against William?
4. Copy the table on the right. Use Source **F** to fill it in.

The armies at Hastings

	Weapons and armour	Usefulness in battle
Housecarls		
Fyrd		
Knights		
Archers		

The Battle of Hastings

As the day began on 14 October Harold's army was still moving into position. He stood on the centre of the long ridge of Senlac Hill. Next to Harold fluttered his battle flags – the dragon of Wessex and his own banner, the fighting man. Around him stood the best of his troops, the housecarls, holding their deadly axes. To his left and right were the fyrd, with their makeshift weapons. It was a strong position. What can we learn from the evidence about William's attack?

Source G William prepares for battle. Written by Orderic Vitalis, a Norman monk, in about 1130.

> William heard mass and hung from his neck the holy relics on which Harold had sworn. He drew up his archers in the first line; the infantry in armour formed the second rank; behind them came the cavalry, the flower of his troops, with William in the centre of them.

Source H The Normans attack Harold's army. Written by William of Poitiers in about 1071. He was not at the battle.

> Duke William and his men came slowly up the hill, raining death upon the English with their arrows. The English fought back bravely hurling weapons of all kinds. The knights crashed into the enemy but they held steady behind their wall of shields, their axes cutting through Norman shields and armour. For a long time the battle raged then the Normans heard that their leader was dead and began to run.
>
> William thrust himself to the front of them shouting and threatening them with his spear, 'Look. I am still alive and with God's help I will be the winner yet'. Fired by these words the Normans turned on the English who had chased them and cut them down so that none got away.

Source I The Bayeux Tapestry, showing the English defending Senlac Hill

Source J The Bayeux Tapestry, showing Norman knights charging a wall of English shields

Source K The Normans win the battle. Written by William of Poitiers in about 1071.

> Heartened by their success, the Normans attacked again and this time pretended to retreat. As before, several thousand English chased them, but the Normans suddenly turned their horses and cut them down. Twice this trick was used with complete success. Still the English fought on stubbornly until there were more dead than living. As evening fell, exhausted and beaten, they began to run as swiftly as they could.

Source L From the *Anglo-Saxon Chronicle*

> William took Harold by surprise before his men were ready for battle. Even so, the king fought hard against him and each side suffered heavy losses. King Harold and his brothers, Leofwine and Gyrth, and many good men were slain.

Source M The Bayeux tapestry showing the death of Harold. The writing is in Latin. It says 'Here King Harold was killed'.

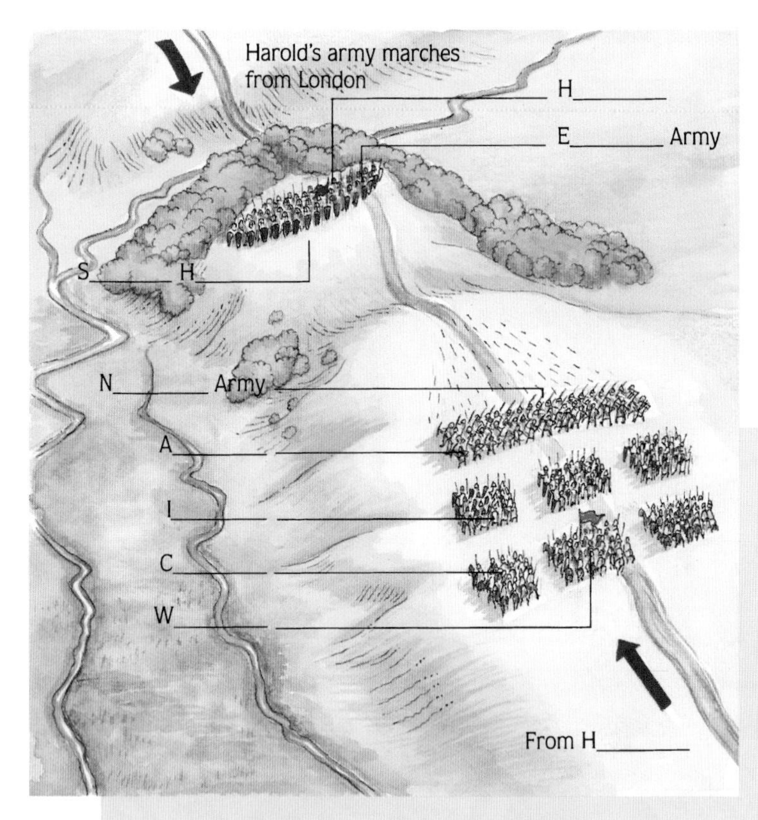

Investigations

1 Copy the sketch map above and finish the labels. Some historians have said Harold chose a good place to fight. Do you agree or disagree? Using the map and Sources **H** and **I** on page 13, explain why.

2 Using Sources **G, H** and **L** list **three** ways in which William showed himself to be a good general.

3 The evidence on pages 13 and 14 is from **four** different sources. Look back to what you have been told about **three** of them (see pages 8 and 9) and fill in a copy of the following chart.

Name of Source	English or Norman?	How reliable?

4 How is the picture in Source **J** useful to someone writing about the fighting at the Battle of Hastings?

5 Look at Sources **H**, **L** and **M**. What do they tell us about the importance of leaders in battles? Why was it unlucky for England that Harold's brothers were killed too?

6 Draw a sketch map to show the position of the armies at the end of the Battle of Hastings.

Remember...

- **William of Normandy invaded England in 1066.**
- **He won the Battle of Hastings, and King Harold was killed.**

Depth Study: William takes power

- ***How did William crush English resistance?***
- ***How did the English fight back?***

Taking the throne

The day after the Battle of Hastings the Norman invaders were still in a dangerous situation. William knew that if he gave the English time to recover they might gather another army or choose another king. William acted quickly and ruthlessly, while the English argued about what to do next.

Source A An account of William's generosity. Written by William of Poitiers in about 1071.

William marched to Dover where the English, stricken with fear, prepared to surrender. But our men, greedy for loot, set fire to the castle. The Duke, unwilling that those who had offered to give up should suffer loss gave them money for the damage. Having captured the castle the Duke spent eight days making it stronger.

Source B William strikes hard. Written by Florence of Worcester in about 1115.

Aldred Archbishop of York, the people of London and Earls Edwin and Morcar planned to put Prince Edgar [a cousin of Edward the Confessor] on the throne. But while many were preparing to fight, the Earls went home with their army. Meanwhile Duke William was **laying waste** Sussex, Kent, Hampshire, Middlesex and Hertfordshire, burning villages and slaughtering the inhabitants. He was then met by Edwin and Morcar and the leading men of London who **submitted** to him.

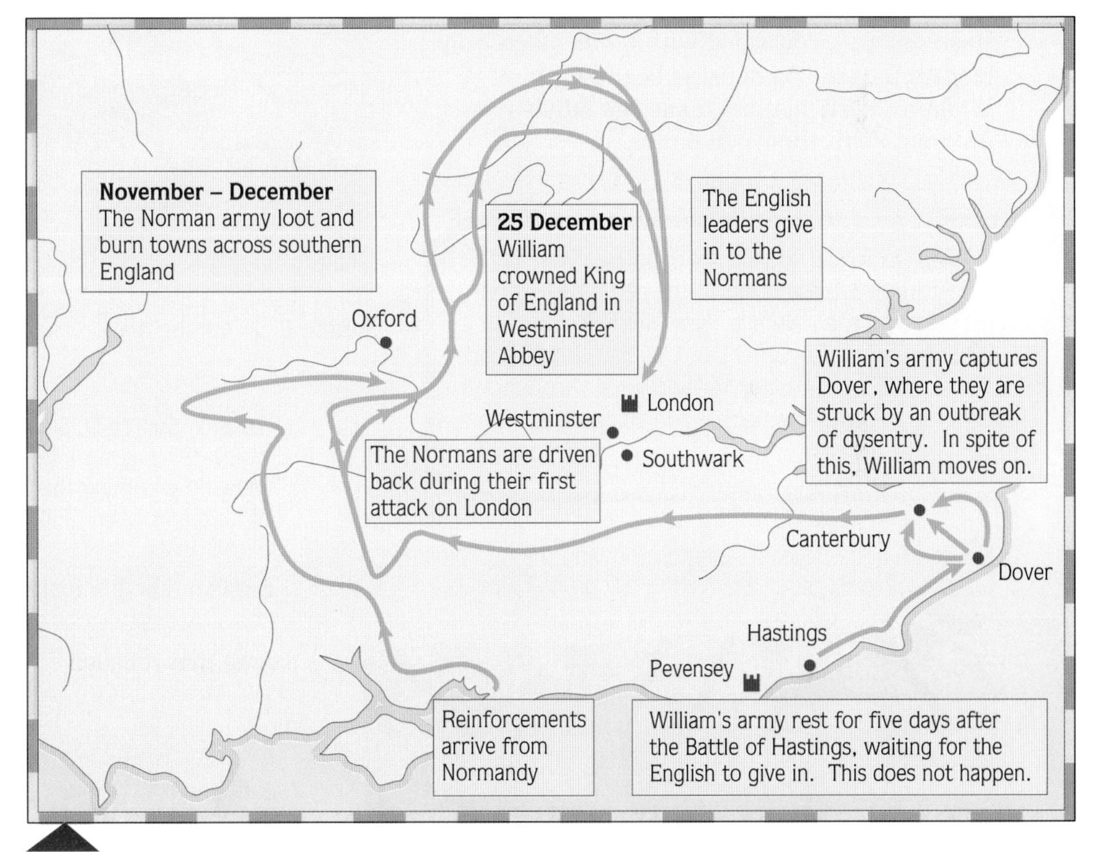

Source C
William's march on London

1. Copy the outline of southern England in Source **C**. Read Source **B** and shade in the counties William attacked. Use Source **E** on page 7 to help you.
2. Compare Sources **A** and **B**. Why do you think William was kind to the English in Dover but so cruel as he marched towards London?
3. How did Edwin and Morcar behave in Source **B**? Why do you think they did this?

Key words

Dysentery A disease causing severe diarrhoea.
Lay waste Rob and destroy.
Submitted Agreed to accept him as king.

William's coronation – a bad omen

On Christmas Day 1066 William was crowned King of England in Westminster Abbey. The English and Normans swore to serve the new king and cheered him so loudly that Norman troops on guard thought there was a riot and burned down nearby houses. This was a grim beginning for William. It showed the deep distrust that remained between the conquerors and the conquered. For the next five years the Normans had to crush repeated rebellions and invasions.

William I – a hard ruler

William set about ruling England with a firm hand. Castles were built in important cities. The Norman barons who had helped him win at Hastings were rewarded with lands taken from English thegns. As Sources **B** and **C** show, William's early actions made the English unhappy with their new king.

Source D Threats to William 1067–1070

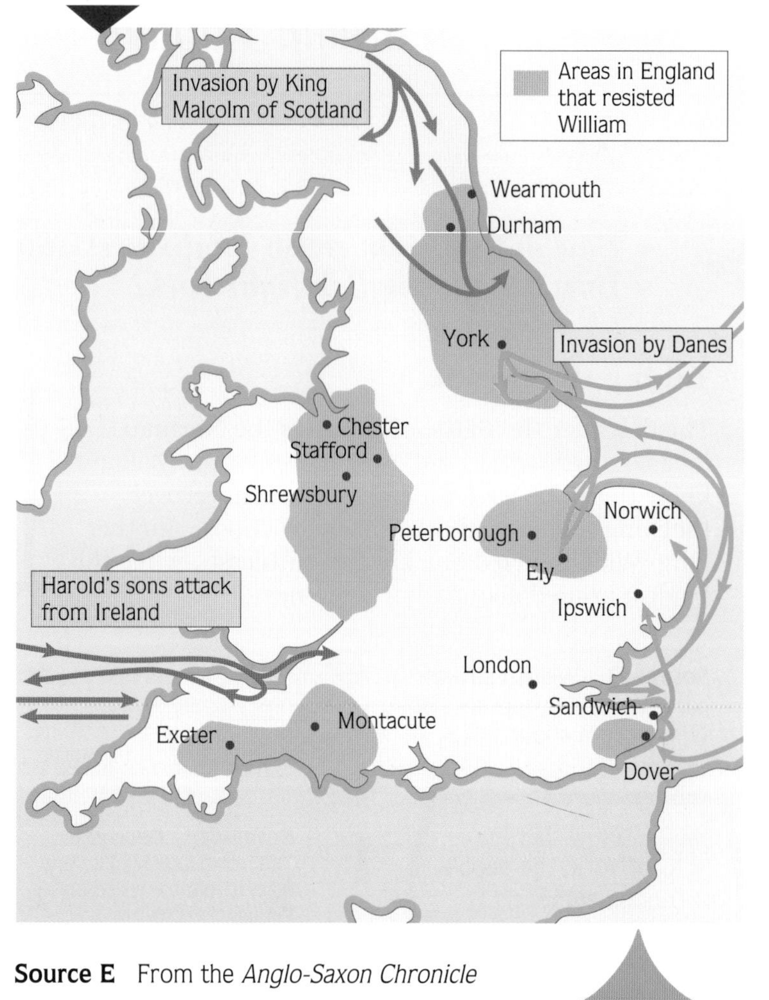

William promised to rule his people as well as the best kings before him. All the same he laid on heavy taxes and then went to Normandy leaving Bishop Odo [his half brother] and William Fitz Osborn in charge. They built castles far and wide throughout the land, oppressing the people and things went from bad to worse.

Source E From the *Anglo-Saxon Chronicle*

Investigations

1 Look at Source **D**. Some areas of the country were more likely to rebel than others. Why do you think this was? (Clue: Where are they? Who might help?) Fill in the following chart.

English rebellions against William

Area that rebelled	Reasons
1	
2	
3	
4	
5	

2 Draw an outline map of England. You have to build 25 castles for William. Where will you put them? Write a caption explaining your reasons. Compare your plans with what really happened by looking at Source **K** on page 22.

3 Look at the text and Sources **E** and **F**. What might a Norman have thought about what William was doing? What might an English person have said?

Source F The Bayeux Tapestry, showing the first Norman castle built in England. Many others soon followed.

The English fight back

In 1067 the first rebellion against the Normans was led by Edric the Wild in Herefordshire. This sparked off other revolts in Kent. The following year the city of Exeter rebelled. William dealt with these with a mixture of firmness and mercy. But his patience was wearing thin when the worst crisis broke in 1068–9.

The north was the most independent part of England. When William tried to raise taxes and send in Norman lords this led to a widespread uprising in the north to put Prince Edgar on the throne. William crushed this in 1068 and left troops stationed in two new castles at York. To his fury the rebels rose again in 1069, this time with Danish support.

Source G The rebellion in the north. From the *Anglo-Saxon Chronicle.*

William gave Northumberland to Earl Robert but the people of Durham massacred the earl and 900 soldiers. Prince Edgar and the rebels came to York and the people of the city joined them. William came from the south and surprised them, ravaging York and killing hundreds. Then the Danes came with 240 ships into the Humber and joined the English leaders. With a huge and joyful army they stormed York, killed hundreds of Normans, burned the castle and captured a vast treasure.

William came to York only to learn that the Danes had fled. The king ordered his men to repair the castles. He set out to search the forests and remote mountains, stopping at nothing to hunt down the rebels hidden there. He cut down many, destroyed the lairs of others and burned homes. Nowhere else had William shown such cruelty. His fury was blind and he punished the innocent with the guilty. He ordered that all crops, herds and food be burned, so that the whole region north of the Humber had nothing to live on.

Source H William's revenge. By Orderic Vitalis, written in about 1130.

Source I The Bayeux Tapestry, showing Normans burning a house

There was so great a famine that men ate human flesh and horses, dogs and cats. Some sold themselves into slavery while others died on the roads. Corpses rotted in the streets because there was no one to bury them.

Source J Famine in the north. By Symeon of Durham, a monk, writing in the early 1100s.

William crushes English resistance

Throughout the winter of 1069–70 William led his army across the north of England burning houses and killing people. When he had finished, the area was a blackened waste. Although Hereward the Wake fought on around Ely, the last real threat to the Norman conquest had been wiped out. The effects of the damage William caused lasted for many years (Source **K**). He may have believed he was dealing with rebels and disloyal traitors (Source **L**), but there is some evidence that his merciless actions troubled him on his death bed. (Source **J**).

Source K
Twenty years after William's punishment of the north, many villages were still wasteland

Source L William deals with the English. By William of Malmesbury, writing in about 1135.

> At times the king was quite severe with the English, for he found hardly any of them loyal. This angered him and he took from the greater of them first their wealth, then their land and finally, in some cases, their lives.

Source M William's deathbed confession. By Orderic Vitalis, in about 1130. Orderic was not there and is giving his own opinion on what William said.

> I fell on the northern shires like a hungry lion. I ordered their houses and corn with all their tools and goods to be burnt and great herds of cattle to be butchered. I took my revenge by giving them famine. Alas, I kept the throne by so many crimes.

Remember...

- **William was faced with threats from all sides after 1066.**
- **The rebellion in the north was the most serious and William smashed it ruthlessly.**

Investigations

1 Copy and complete the following table. You will find the information in the sources given.

The crushing of the north 1068–70

Causes of the rebellion (text and Source **G**) ____________

English actions (Source **G**) ____________

William's actions (Sources **G**, **H** and **I**) ____________

Results (Sources **J** and **K**) ____________

2 Historians have said that William punished the people in the north to teach the whole country a lesson. Explain what this means.

3 Look at Sources **J** and **M**. How did William use famine as a weapon? What were the advantages and disadvantages of this?

4 How do the writers of Sources **L** and **M** agree and disagree in their views of William's actions?

Keeping a kingdom

How did William keep control of England?

The feudal system

By 1071 William was master of England. But how was he to stay in charge? His answer was in what he did with the land. William claimed that because he had conquered England, all the country now belonged to him. He used some of this to buy the loyalty and support of the great Norman barons who had helped him in his invasion. William **granted** them huge estates. In return, they agreed to help him rule England by controlling the local people, collecting taxes and fighting for him. This is known as the feudal system. It affected the lives of everyone in the country (Source **A**).

Source A
The feudal system

The king
Promises to rule well
Grants land to barons and bishops

Barons and bishops (about 300)
Services: Loyalty to the king
Supply knights for the army for about 40 days a year
Control local people
Collect taxes
Barons grant land to their knights and promise them protection and justice

Knights (about 4000)
Services: Loyalty to their lord
Fight on his orders for 40 days a year
Knights grant land to their peasants and promise them protection and justice

Peasants (about 1.5 million)
Services: Obey their lord
Work on his land
Pay taxes

Source B
A knight swears loyalty to his lord

Key words

Grant Not a gift. A strong king like William could take the land away again.

Remember...

- **The feudal system was an exchange of land for services.**

Investigations

1 Copy the following statements and match each statement to the right person.

King	Baron	Knight	Peasant

- *I must work on my lord's land.*
- *I own all the land.*
- *I grant land to my knights.*
- *I must fight for 40 days a year when my lord orders.*

Make up one comment of your own for each person.

2 'The feudal system made sure everyone had a master'. Use Source **A** to explain this statement.

3 How does Source **B** show that swearing loyalty was an important ceremony? How important was loyalty to the feudal system?

4 Look back to Source **D** on page 6. Do you think England had something like the feudal system before 1066? Why?

The English lose their lands

At first, William was content to allow English earls to keep their lands – if they were loyal to him. He gave Norman knights the lands of English thegns who had been killed in the battles of 1066. Later, William took the land and property of English earls who were not loyal to him. Innocent people were driven off their lands by force. By 1086 nearly all farmlands and villages had been taken by the Normans.

The Domesday Book

In 1085 William had to raise an army to stop an invasion from Norway. He paid for this by raising taxes from the English. In 1086 William sent out officials to visit 13 000 villages in England. They collected details of what land and property everybody owned. Only the counties in the far north and a few large towns such as London were missed out. Their findings were gathered together in two great volumes known as the Domesday Book. William used these to decide how much tax people should pay.

Source C The English thegns lose their land to the Normans

The Normans had taken the land from the English landowners in each area of the country by the dates given on the map

Scotland
1090
1070
1071
1070–80
Wales
London
1068–70
1067–8

Source D What William's officials wanted to find out about each village

The Book of Judgement

The Domesday Book was given its name by the English. To them, the work of William's officials seemed like the Day of Judgement (or 'Doom's Day') when God was to make an account of people's actions during their lives.

The book gave details of who held the land in England in 1086. From this we can see how far the Normans had taken over by then.

Only 2 of the 180 biggest landowners were English. From the information in the Domesday Book, we can build up a clear picture of life in England in the early Middle Ages.

Source E The Domesday Book for Dedham in Essex

Roger de Raismes holds Dedham. In 1066 there were 7 villagers, now 5; always 24 smallholders. Then 4 slaves, now 3. Then the lord had 2 ploughs, now 3. Then the men had 10 ploughs, now 5. There is woodland enough for 250 pigs; 40 acres of meadow; then 1 mill, now 2; then 5 cows, now 3; then 40 sheep, now 100; then 25 pigs, now 30. Value always £12.

Source F Who held the land in England in 1086?

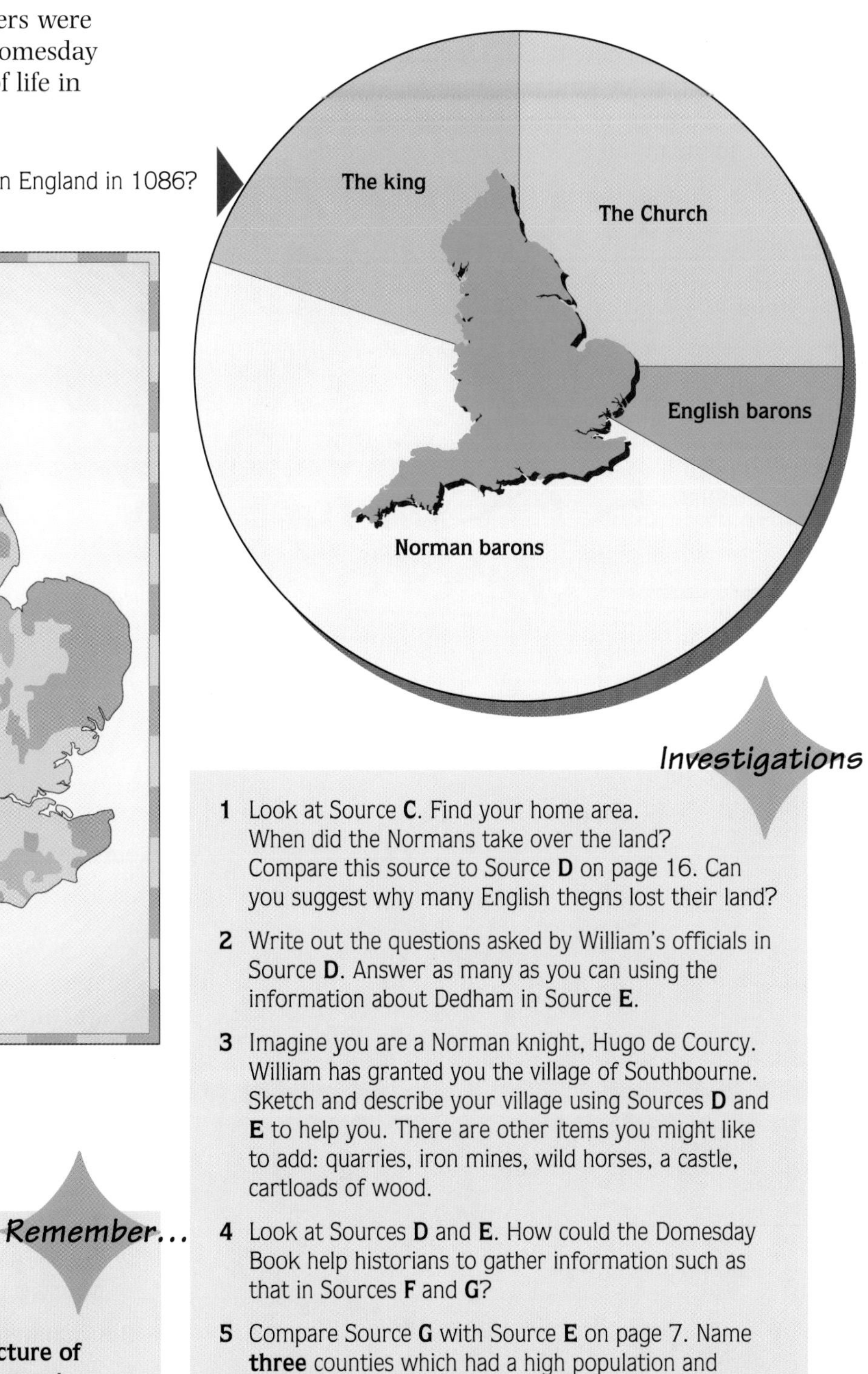

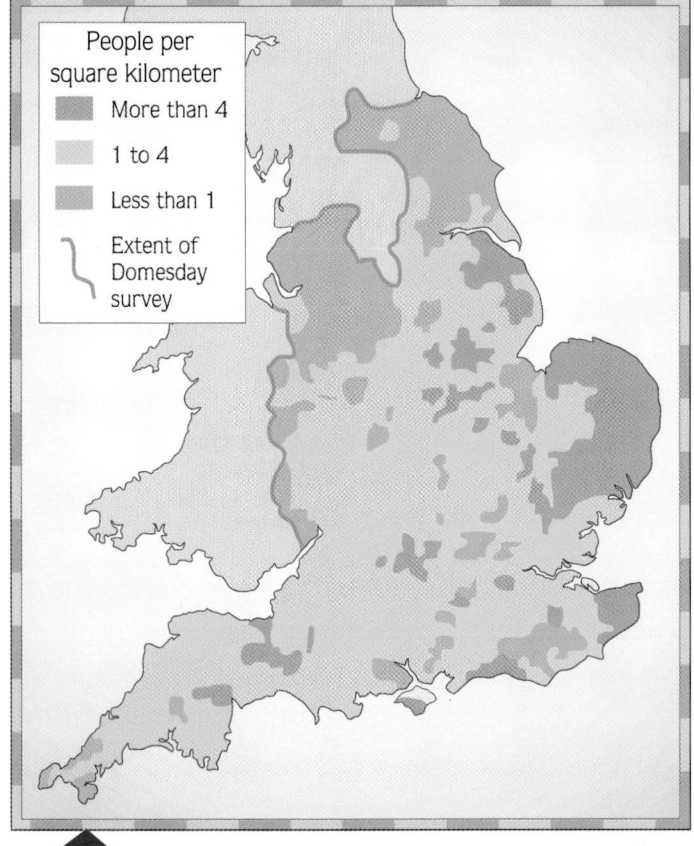

Source G Where people lived in England in 1086, according to the Domesday survey

Remember...

- **The feudal system helped William to reward his barons and keep control of England.**
- **The Domesday Book gives us a clear picture of England 20 years after the Norman Conquest.**

Investigations

1. Look at Source **C**. Find your home area. When did the Normans take over the land? Compare this source to Source **D** on page 16. Can you suggest why many English thegns lost their land?
2. Write out the questions asked by William's officials in Source **D**. Answer as many as you can using the information about Dedham in Source **E**.
3. Imagine you are a Norman knight, Hugo de Courcy. William has granted you the village of Southbourne. Sketch and describe your village using Sources **D** and **E** to help you. There are other items you might like to add: quarries, iron mines, wild horses, a castle, cartloads of wood.
4. Look at Sources **D** and **E**. How could the Domesday Book help historians to gather information such as that in Sources **F** and **G**?
5. Compare Source **G** with Source **E** on page 7. Name **three** counties which had a high population and **three** which had a low population in 1086.

Source H Orderic Vitalis, in about 1130

> The strongholds which the French call castles were very few in England and for this reason the English, though warlike and brave, were too weak to resist their enemies.

Castles

Castles were common in Normandy before 1066. They were small, strong forts. They were difficult to attack without special equipment. Castles were ideal as a base for controlling the surrounding countryside. When the Normans invaded England they brought the idea with them (see Source **F** page 16).

Some castles were built to protect William's troops. Others were built by Norman barons or knights to protect their families and followers as they took over their new lands. The first castles were the motte and bailey kind (see page 5). These were wooden towers, or keeps, built on top of small hills or man-made mounds. Many of these were later rebuilt with stone.

Source I A motte and bailey castle. A castle like this could be built in two weeks.

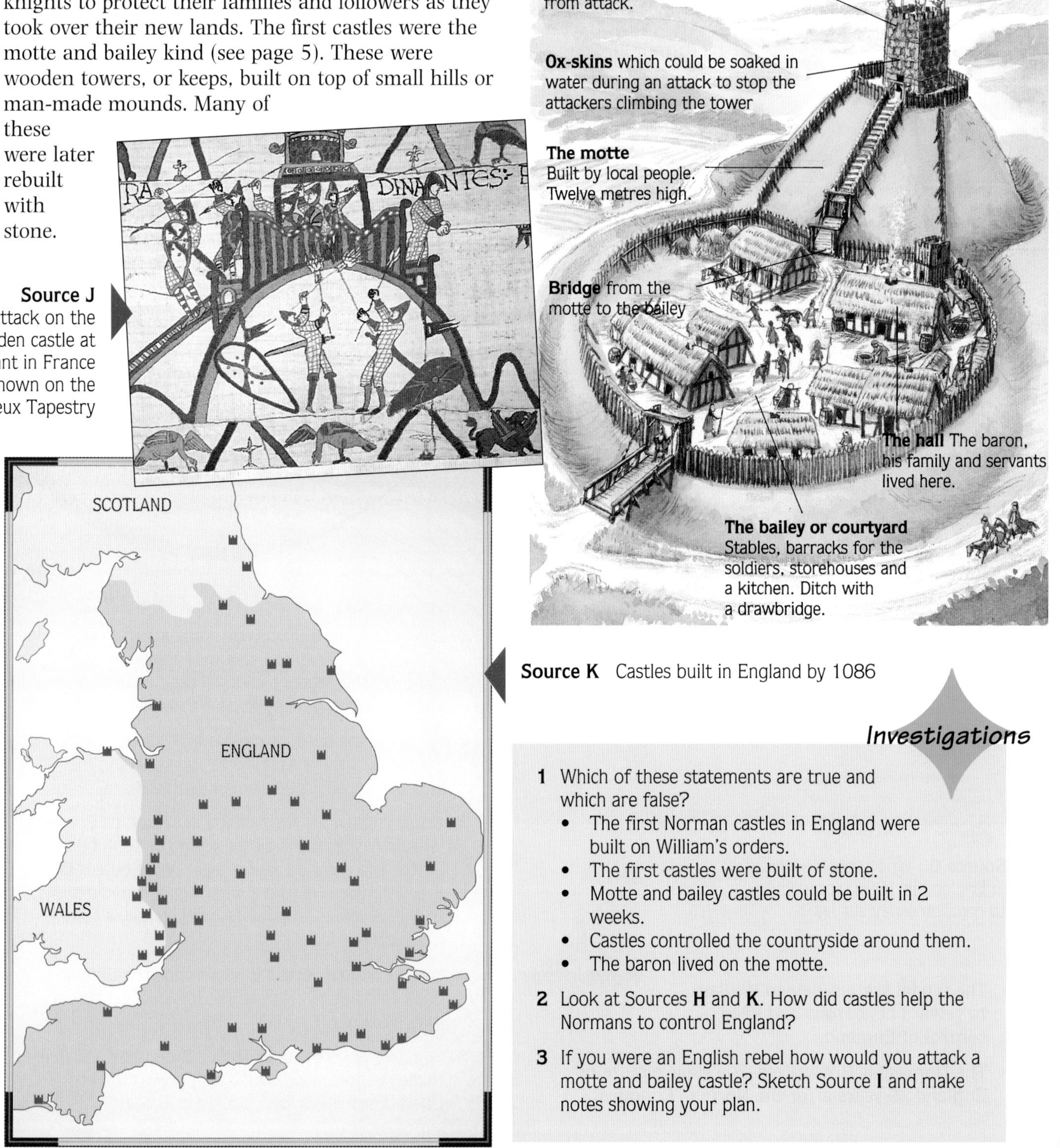

Source J An attack on the wooden castle at Dinant in France shown on the Bayeux Tapestry

Source K Castles built in England by 1086

Investigations

1. Which of these statements are true and which are false?
   - The first Norman castles in England were built on William's orders.
   - The first castles were built of stone.
   - Motte and bailey castles could be built in 2 weeks.
   - Castles controlled the countryside around them.
   - The baron lived on the motte.
2. Look at Sources **H** and **K**. How did castles help the Normans to control England?
3. If you were an English rebel how would you attack a motte and bailey castle? Sketch Source **I** and make notes showing your plan.

Verdict on William

William the Conqueror died in 1087. There is no doubt that he was an able king. However, there are different opinions about his character and achievements, as Sources **L–O** show.

Source M An English view of William, from the *Anglo-Saxon Chronicle*. This was written shortly after William's death.

> He was a very wise man. He was stronger than any king before him and stern to those who resisted him. He built castles, which was hard on poor men. He was greedy and taxed his subjects too heavily. Yet we must not forget that he kept good order in the land, so that an honest man could travel unharmed.

Source N A Norman view of William, written by a monk in Normandy in about 1190

> He was a strong and tall man who never backed away from a challenge because it was hard or dangerous. He was a clear speaker, good at persuading others to do what he wanted.

Source O A modern opinion of William, written in 1981. From *English Historical Documents* by David Douglas and George Greenaway.

> William was a strong and pitiless king – a man to fear rather than love. But he was not a **tyrant**. The English felt the harshness of his rule, but later came to feel pride in their conqueror. He dominated his age and permanently changed the course of English history.

Remember...

- **The Normans used castles to control the English.**
- **Early castles were built of wood.**
- **There are differing views about whether William was a good king.**

Key words

Tyrant A cruel ruler.

Source L William I ('William the Conqueror') and his descendants

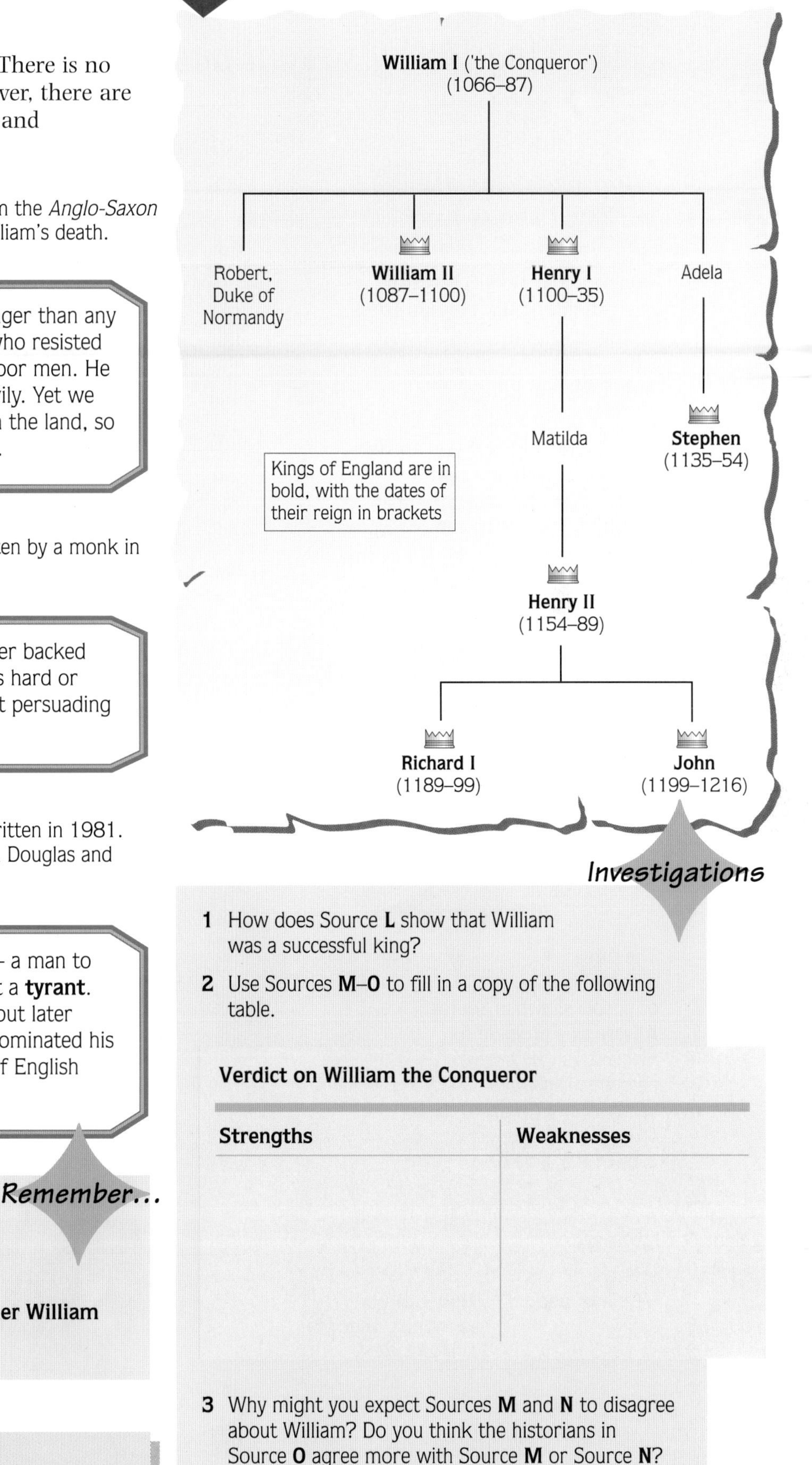

Investigations

1 How does Source **L** show that William was a successful king?

2 Use Sources **M–O** to fill in a copy of the following table.

Verdict on William the Conqueror

Strengths	Weaknesses

3 Why might you expect Sources **M** and **N** to disagree about William? Do you think the historians in Source **O** agree more with Source **M** or Source **N**?

2 The medieval monarch – power and its problems

King Henry's nightmare

What problems did medieval kings face?

The king was the most powerful person in the country. He had to defend England and keep law and order. But the power of the king was always being threatened.

Henry I became king in 1100 and had to fight hard to hold on to his kingdom. One night he had a terrifying dream in which he was attacked by three groups of enemies. His nightmare (Source **A**) shows the kinds of people every king had to control during the Middle Ages. In this chapter we look at some of the problems kings had to face.

Source A Pictures of King Henry's nightmare drawn by John of Worcester in the twelfth century. John was a friend of the king's doctor.

Investigations

The three different groups of people shown in Source **A** were all a problem for medieval kings: angry peasants, churchmen and barons. Look closely at the pictures and complete a copy of the table below.

Henry's Nightmare

	Type of people	How can we recognise them in the pictures?
Picture 1		
Picture 2		
Picture 3		

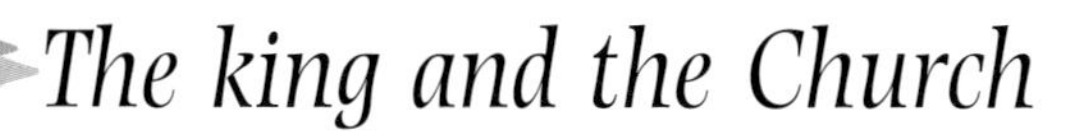

The king and the Church

Why was the Archbishop of Canterbury murdered in 1170?

On 29 December 1170 four knights hacked Thomas Becket, the most important Church leader in England, to death. They claimed they were acting on the orders of King Henry II. How could this tragedy have happened?

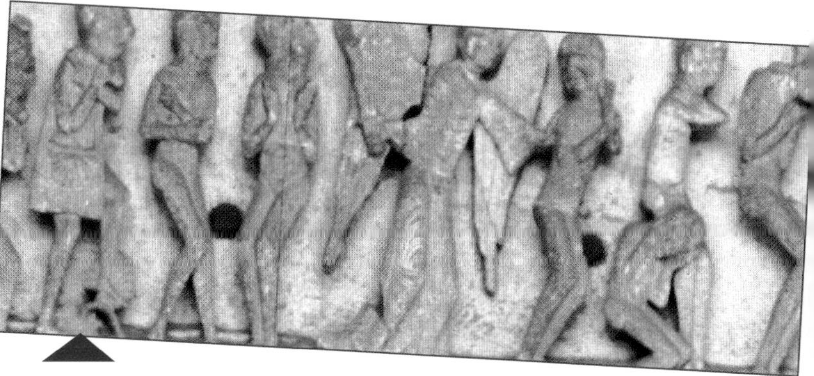

Source A An angel sorting souls. Those on the left are saved. Those on the right are being sent to hell. This scene was carved over the door of the Cathedral in Autun in France in the twelfth century.

Why was the Archbishop of Canterbury important?

The church was the most important building in any town or village. It was the centre of the community. Priests took care of people while they were alive and made sure their souls went to heaven after their death.

All the countries of Western Europe, including England, were Christian and part of the Roman Catholic **Church**. The leader of the Church was the Pope, who lived in Rome. Most people believed that the Pope was God's servant on earth and in matters of religion his word was law.

Source B The coronation of a king. The king was thought to be chosen by God. He needed the blessing of the Church at his coronation. This picture shows the coronation of King Edward I.

The Pope's power reached out from Rome through a network of archbishops and bishops, each in charge of an area called a diocese. They were rich men, usually well educated and from noble families. The most powerful person in England after the king was the Archbishop of Canterbury. The king could choose the Archbishop, but the Church had its own laws and courts. Even the king sometimes had to obey the Pope.

Key words

Church This can mean a church building or an entire Christian community – such as the Roman Catholic Church.

Investigations

1. Of the five statements below, two are false. Write out the three true ones.
   - The Pope lived in England.
   - The Pope was head of the Roman Catholic Church.
   - The Roman Catholic Church was a large building in Rome.
   - People believed the Church helped them get to heaven.
   - Bishops passed on the orders of the Pope.
2. Look carefully at Source **A**. How would this idea about what happened after death make people obey the Church?
3. How does Source **B** show the importance of the Church – even for kings?

What was Henry II like?

Henry became king in 1154. He took over a country in ruins. The feeble government of King Stephen had let the barons get out of control. They had built castles without permission, fought each other and stolen land from weaker men.

Henry had to bring back order. He had great energy and was always on the move around his kingdom. He was a good army leader, and forced the barons to obey him. He took back royal lands and castles that Stephen had lost.

Courts run by barons and sheriffs had become dishonest. Arguments about land had been settled in combat, where the strongest fighter won. Henry appointed honest royal judges who toured the country. He ordered that cases about land be settled in royal courts. He returned stolen lands to their rightful owners. Ordinary people used the king's court because they were fairer. The money from court fines went to the king, so this meant he needed to raise less in taxes.

Source C Henry's kingdom in 1175. In a reign of 32 years he spent Christmas in 24 different places.

Source D Two views of Henry II's character

The king's eyes are dove-like when he is at peace, but in bursts of temper they flash like lightening. He never sits down except when on horseback or at meals. He always has his weapons in his hands when not working or at his books.

By Peter Blois, a scholar who travelled with Henry's court

He was fierce to those who challenged him, but merciful to those he defeated; hard on his servants and generous with strangers. If he hated someone he hardly ever came to love them: if he loved someone he hardly ever came to hate them.

Written by Gerald of Wales, a bishop, in the 1180s

Source E The royal seal of Henry II. This was stamped in wax on his orders.

Henry II and Thomas Becket

Thomas Becket was the son of a London merchant. He was very talented and rose quickly to become Chancellor in 1154. This was a vital job. He was in charge of the men who wrote the king's letters and sent out his orders. During this time he became Henry's trusted friend. They worked, hunted, got drunk and chased women together.

Why did Henry and Thomas quarrel?

In 1162 Henry made Becket Archbishop of Canterbury. He thought this was the perfect way of getting control of the Church. But to Henry's disappointment, Thomas took his duties seriously (Source **F**).

In 1164 the king complained that priests who committed crimes were being let off too lightly by Church courts. He wanted them treated the same as everyone else and sent to royal courts. When Becket refused, the king ordered that he be put on trial. Hearing this, Thomas fled abroad.

In 1170 Henry used the Archbishop of York to crown his eldest son. The king believed this was vital to stop any fighting over who should be the next ruler after his death. It was important for Henry to show that the next king had the approval and blessing of the Church. He also invited Thomas to come back.

Becket returned but was furious. He excommunicated all the bishops who had been helping Henry while he was away. As Source **G** shows, the scene was set for a tragedy.

Source F Becket's character. By C. Warren Holister, from *The Making of England, 1988.*

> Becket changed from a chancellor who enjoyed life to a stern archbishop. He felt it his duty to stand up for the rights of God's Church. Other churchmen thought he did not deserve the job, so he wore a **hair shirt** under his clothes to show his devotion to God. He would not be Henry's tool.

Source G By William Fitzstephen, a priest in Becket's household, writing in 1175

> The Archbishop of York and other bishops met the king and told him they had been **excommunicated**. They said Becket was a traitor, going around England at the head of a strong army. One of them said, 'My lord, while Thomas lives you will not see peace or quiet or have good days'. At this the king felt great anger against Becket. Four knights eager to win his favour left the court to kill the Archbishop.

Murder in the cathedral

We know the details of Becket's murder because eyewitnesses wrote down what they saw. One was Edward Grim, a priest who tried to save Thomas.

> The murderers came in full armour with swords and axes. The monks tried to bolt the doors against them but the Archbishop ordered them to be opened, saying 'It is not right to make a fortress of a house of prayer'. In a mad fury the knights called out 'Where is Thomas Becket, traitor to the king and the country?' He replied, 'I am ready to die for my God so that my blood will win the Church peace and freedom'. They tried to drag him outside to kill him but he clung to a pillar. Then, realising that he was to die, he bowed his head in prayer and joined his hands together. The first blow struck his head and almost cut off the arm of him who tells the story, for he had his arms around the Archbishop to protect him. The second blow also struck his head but he stood firm. At the third blow he fell to his knees and elbows.The fourth blow split his skull and his blood and brains stained the floor.

Source I An eyewitness account of Becket's murder, by Edward Grim

Key words

Hair shirt A shirt of very rough cloth to make the wearer uncomfortable.
Excommunicate Expel from the Church.

Source H A painting made in about 1180. Four knights arrive while Becket sits at supper. They kill him but later return to pray at his tomb.

Who won – the Church or the king?

The Church	The king
Henry apologised and allowed himself to be whipped in public by monks. Becket was made a saint in 1173 by the Pope. Pilgrims flocked to see his tomb (and still do). Criminal priests were still tried in Church courts.	Henry could still choose Archbishops. The Pope needed to stay friends with Henry. When things cooled down he let the king keep tight control over the Church.

Source J This picture of the murder of Becket was painted in about 1190. How far does it back up the evidence of Edward Grim's eyewitness account in Source I?

Remember...

- **Henry was a dynamic king who gave England strong government.**
- **He wanted to control the Church but was stopped by his old friend Thomas Becket, Archbishop of Canterbury.**
- **Four knights killed Thomas to please the king.**

Investigations

1. Look at Source **C**. Why might Henry have needed to travel round his kingdom so much?
2. Read Source **D**. Do you think Henry had the right character to be a successful king? If you could give him advice, what would you say? Begin like this:

   Your majesty, may I humbly suggest...
3. Becket was in charge of Source **E**. How does this show that Henry trusted him?
4. Read Source **F**. Is a historian more or less likely to give a fair view of Becket's character than someone who lived at the time? Give reasons for your answer.
5. According to Source **G**, how guilty was the king for Becket's death?
6. Some historians have said that Becket wanted to die. According to Sources **H** and **I** do you think this is true? Why might Becket think dying would help his cause?

The king and the barons

Why did King John sign Magna Carta?

On Monday morning, 15 June 1215, King John met his barons on a meadow at Runnymede near Windsor. Only a month before, their rebel army had captured London. Faced with a civil war he was likely to lose, John signed the Great Charter or Magna Carta. This was a list of 63 demands he had to meet if the barons were to swear their loyalty to him.

Source A Why did the barons rebel against John?

Was John as bad as the barons said?

Historians still argue about whether John was an evil or an unlucky king. **Chroniclers** at the time were monks and had reason to dislike him because of the way he treated the Church (Source **A**). Victorian historians and artists based their work on these writers and their view of 'bad King John' is still very popular, especially with TV and film makers. (Sources **C**, **D** and **E**). Some modern historians are less critical (Source **F**).

Source B King John – a thirteenth century view. By Matthew Paris, a thirteenth-century monk.

> He was a tyrant crushing his own people. He lost Normandy and many other territories. He was a greedy money grabber. Hell is too good for a foul person like him.

Source C King John – a Victorian view, from *Short History of the English People*, 1877, by J.R. Green

> John was the worst of his family. Their wickedness, insolence, selfishness, uncontrolled lust, cruelty and tyranny, shamelessness, superstition and dislike of truth or honour were concentrated in him.

Key words

Chronicler An early historian.

Source D Part of a nineteenth-century painting showing John signing the Magna Carta. The original hangs in the House of Commons.

Source E
King John as portrayed in the film *The Adventures of Robin Hood*

Source F John's good points. By C. Warren Hollister, from *The Making of England*, 1988.

John had some triumphs. He won battles against the Scottish and Welsh. The Irish accepted him as their overlord. He gave England a well organised navy. He enforced the law strongly and justly – unless there was something in it for him. He had to raise taxes because his brother Richard left him with an empty treasury.

1 Copy this spidergram. Use Sources **A** and **B** to explain John's bad points.

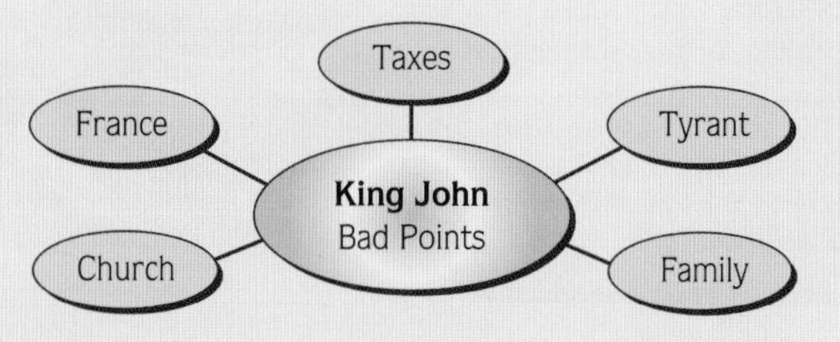

Which of these bad points do you think is the worst? Explain why.

2 Using Source **F**, draw a similar diagram showing John's good points.

3 Why must we be careful when we read sources like Source **B** about King John?

4 How can we tell that the author of Source **C** did not like John's family? In what ways did John behave the same as his father?

5 Describe how John is shown in Sources **D** and **E**. How will pictures like this affect peoples' opinions of him?

6 Why do you think TV and film makers like to show John as a black-hearted villain rather than a king with good and bad points?

Was Magna Carta a failure?

Magna Carta has been called the 'Charter of Liberty' because it was the first time that the rights and freedoms of English people were written down.

This wasn't what the barons wanted. Most of the points in the Charter were about their rights and privileges. They believed the king was not playing his part in the feudal system and they were trying to make it work properly again. A few demands concerned other people who might be useful allies to the barons, such as the Church and merchants. The Charter only covered free men, but most English people were not free – they were **villeins**.

Within weeks John claimed he had been forced to sign Magna Carta, and so it was worthless. England collapsed into civil war until John's death in 1216. However, in the years that followed, the Charter became more important. It was re-issued by other kings in the thirteenth century and became part of the law. In later centuries it inspired people who were struggling for their freedom, especially the Americans when they broke away from the British Empire in 1776.

Source G Some of the main points in Magna Carta

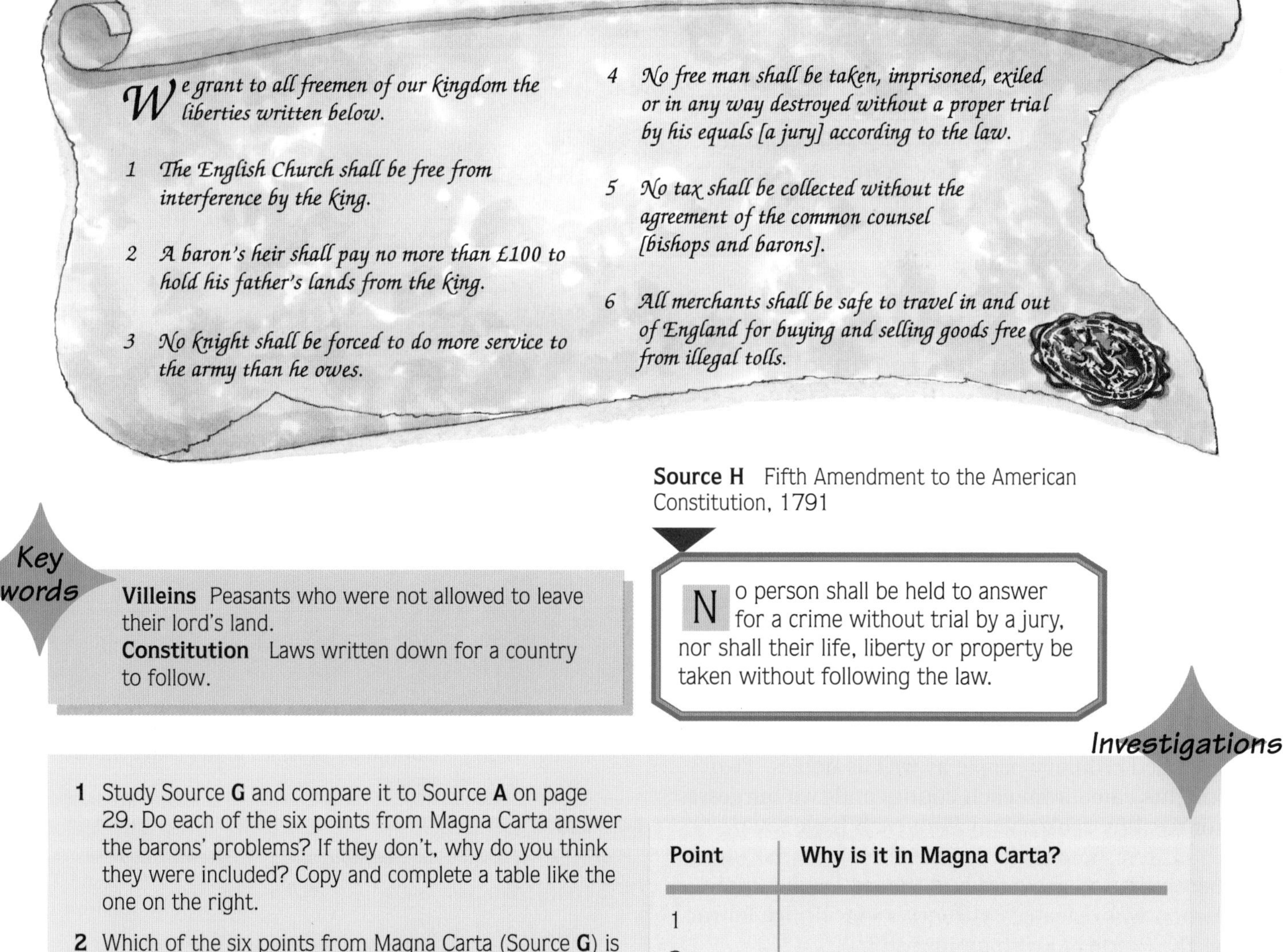

We grant to all freemen of our kingdom the liberties written below.

1 *The English Church shall be free from interference by the king.*

2 *A baron's heir shall pay no more than £100 to hold his father's lands from the king.*

3 *No knight shall be forced to do more service to the army than he owes.*

4 *No free man shall be taken, imprisoned, exiled or in any way destroyed without a proper trial by his equals [a jury] according to the law.*

5 *No tax shall be collected without the agreement of the common counsel [bishops and barons].*

6 *All merchants shall be safe to travel in and out of England for buying and selling goods free from illegal tolls.*

Source H Fifth Amendment to the American Constitution, 1791

No person shall be held to answer for a crime without trial by a jury, nor shall their life, liberty or property be taken without following the law.

Key words

Villeins Peasants who were not allowed to leave their lord's land.
Constitution Laws written down for a country to follow.

Investigations

1 Study Source **G** and compare it to Source **A** on page 29. Do each of the six points from Magna Carta answer the barons' problems? If they don't, why do you think they were included? Copy and complete a table like the one on the right.

2 Which of the six points from Magna Carta (Source **G**) is similar to Source **H**? What does this show about the influence of Magna Carta on Americans when they drew up their laws 600 years later?

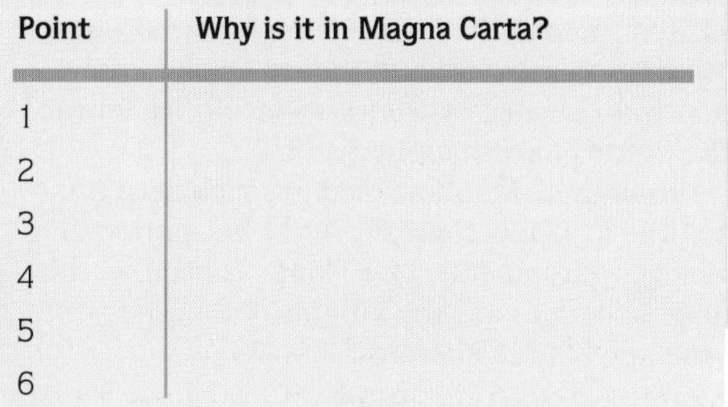

Point	Why is it in Magna Carta?
1	
2	
3	
4	
5	
6	

The king and Parliament

How did Parliament gain power?

Today Parliament is elected by the people and has power over the government. The monarch has little power. In medieval times kings ran the government, but things were beginning to change.

Step 1 – The king asks the barons for advice when he wants it

Controlling a kingdom was not easy. Kings usually listened to advice from their most powerful subjects. Before 1066, English kings had called together the Witan, a council of the most powerful nobles and bishops, to discuss important events. After the Norman Conquest, William the Conqueror continued this idea. His Great Council met three times a year at Christmas, Easter and Whitsuntide to discuss his plans.

Step 2 – The king has to consult the barons – and ordinary people are included

As you have seen, after Magna Carta the king had to get the agreement of the barons if he wanted to raise new taxes. At first, John's son, Henry III, summoned the Great Council regularly and around 1230 these meetings began to be called Parliaments. Later, however, Henry argued with some of his barons and in 1264 they rebelled again. Their leader was Simon de Montfort.

To raise more support Simon decided to call a new kind of Parliament. For the first time it included ordinary people as well as nobles. Two knights came from each county and two burgesses (or wealthy spokesmen) from each large town.

Later, some of the barons thought Simon was becoming too powerful and turned against him. Simon was defeated by Henry's son, Prince Edward, at the Battle of Evesham in 1265.

Although de Montfort died, his idea lived on. When the Prince became Edward I he continued to call bigger Parliaments. Later kings continued this pattern hoping to use the knights and burgesses to cut the power of the barons.

Source A An Anglo-Saxon Witan

Source B Edward I's Parliament

Source C Changes in the king's money

1130	
Income from own lands	87%
Income from taxes	13%
1272	
Income from own lands	43%
Income from taxes	57%

Step 3 – The power of Parliament grows

Between 1338 and 1453 England was often at war with France. This meant kings like Edward III had to meet the huge costs of raising and supplying their armies. They had to turn to Parliament for new taxes more often.

Before they agreed, Parliament began to ask the king to do something in return and grant their requests, or petitions. These might be about local matters, such as opening a new port, or about national concerns, such as a standard measure for the sale of cloth.

By the 1350s most laws were being made as a result of petitions from Parliament rather than ideas from the king himself. By 1400 it had become the custom for the king to grant new laws before he asked for his taxes.

Source D By 1350 meetings of Parliament settled into a pattern that lasted for centuries

Investigations

1. Compare Sources **A** and **B**. What are the main differences?
2. Look at Source **C** and read Step 3. Explain two reasons why kings needed to call Parliaments more often after about 1250.
3. Read the text and Source **D**. Copy out this table and tick the right box for each sentence. Tick both boxes if things have not changed.

	1350	Now
The king or queen is more powerful than Parliament.	☐	☐
The Commons are elected by the people.	☐	☐
Only the rich have the right to choose who goes to the Commons.	☐	☐
The king or queen must obey Parliament.	☐	☐
Only wealthy people can be chosen to join the Commons.	☐	☐
Parliament meets in two separate groups – Lords and Commons.	☐	☐
Kings or queens don't need to call Parliament unless they are short of money.	☐	☐
Almost anyone can be elected to the Commons.	☐	☐

The king
Ran the government with the help of his advisers. He decided when Parliament was to meet – usually only for a few weeks a year. Parliament could not tell the king what to do, but could stop the payment of taxes if they did not like what he was doing.

Parliament met in two separate groups:

The Lords
The barons and bishops who were regularly invited by the king to attend Parliament became known as the Lords. The right to go to Parliament was passed on from father to son.

The Commons
The knights were chosen to represent their county by other landowners like themselves.

The burgesses were picked by other rich townsmen. They realised they had a lot to gain by working together.

By 1339 they were being called 'men of the Commons'.

Depth Study: The Great Revolt, 1381

Why did the peasants revolt?

The Great Revolt (also known as 'The Peasants' Revolt') shook the roots of medieval life. Some historians see this as the beginning of the end of medieval times. In June 1381 an army of peasants from the south of England marched on London and murdered the king's leading advisers, including the Archbishop of Canterbury. For most of the Middle Ages, ordinary people had little power, but for a few weeks the rich lived in terror. How did this happen?

Source A Disasters. From *The Making of England* by C. Warren Hollister, 1983.

> As the fourteenth century opened life was getting harder. The climate became colder and rainier. There were terrible floods, poor harvests and famine. Then in 1348–49 the Black Death killed at least a third of the population.

Source B The peasants became more important. From *The English 1066–1945* by Christopher Hibbert, 1988.

> Many surviving peasants got more land by taking over the strips of the dead. Others who had no land were able to demand higher wages and if they did not get them run away to another manor or town that would pay.

Source C Landowners used Parliament to cut wages. From the ***Statute** of Labourers*, 1357.

> Evil **servants**, men and women, will not work since the plague without wages two or three times what they were. Now they shall be ordered to serve great men and others for the same wages as they had five years ago or go to prison.

Source D A detail from a sixteenth-century painting showing a man raising his hat to a lady. The nobles still expected peasants to obey them.

Source E Peasants began to question their place in life. From a sermon by John Ball, a poor priest from Kent who became a peasant leader.

> Things cannot go well in England until everything is owned by all the people together, and there is no difference between gentlefolk and peasants. We all come from the same father and mother, Adam and Eve. We are called slaves and are beaten if we do not work. Let us go to the king for he is young and may help.

Source F John Ball at the head of a group of peasants. They are shown carrying the royal flags to show their loyalty to the king. This picture is in Froissart's *Chronicle*.

Source G In 1377–80 the king's advisers introduced new **poll taxes** to pay for wars in France and Scotland. Married men also had to pay the same for their wives.

1377	4d (1p)
1379	4d (1p)
1380	12d (5p)

Source H In 1381 the people of Essex would not pay their taxes. From *The Anonimalle Chronicle* written in York in the late fourteenth century.

Thomas Bampton was sent to Essex to collect unpaid taxes. He threatened the people of Fobbing and they asked for help from villages around them. Banding together the men told Thomas they would not pay a penny. It seemed to them that the taxes were stolen from the poor while the rich paid nothing.

Afterwards 50 000 commoners gathered and went from village to village, burning down the houses of those who would not join them. They captured three of Thomas Bampton's clerks and cut off their heads. All the great lords fled to London.

Remember...

The Great Revolt of 1381 had a number of causes, including the effects of the Black Death and a high poll tax.

Key words

Statute Law.
Servants Workers of all kinds.
Poll tax A tax for which everyone pays the same, no matter what they can afford.

Investigations

1. Compare Sources **A** and **B**. Why might peasants feel they were more important after the Black Death?
2. Look at Sources **E** and **F**. Froissart thought Ball was 'a mad priest'. Why might he have thought this?
3. The poll tax of 1381 brought in less money than that of 1379. Using Sources **G** and **H** can you suggest why?
4. Explain how the Great Revolt happened using these headings to help you. Which do you think was the most important? Why?

Disasters | **Wages** | **Freedom and equality** | **Worried nobles** | **Bad government**

What happened during the Revolt?

The riots in Essex spread across southern England. The peasants demanded freedom and justice, attacking landlords and burning the manorial records that showed the services they owed. As Source **J** shows, many townspeople joined them. Taking up John Ball's idea they decided to go to London to put their complaints to the king. The government was helpless to stop them. The best generals and armies were in Scotland or about to leave for a war in Spain. By 12 June rebel forces of over 50 000 from Essex and Kent were camped outside London. Wat Tyler had been chosen as their leader.

During three days of chaos King Richard II met the rebels and played for time.

Source I Richard II was aged 14 in 1381. The peasants blamed their troubles on his advisers, not on Richard himself.

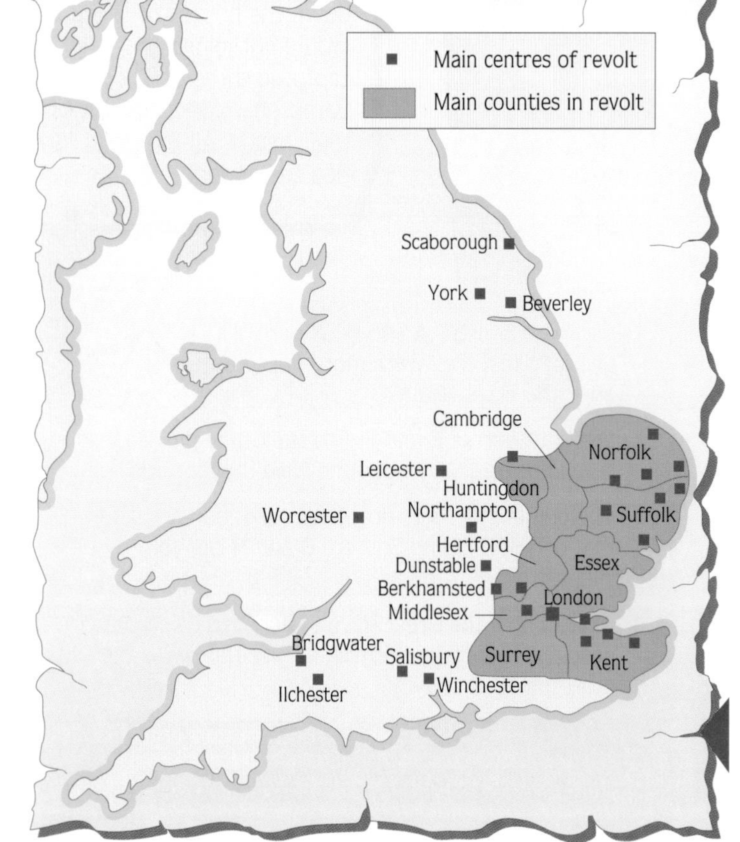

Source J The main counties and towns in the revolt

The events of 13–15 June from *The Anonimalle Chronicle*

13 June

The commons of Southwark forced the guards of London Bridge to let the rebels in. The peasants broke open fleet prison and let the prisoners go. After that they broke open the gates of the palace of John of Gaunt [the king's uncle] and burnt all the buildings inside. Then they besieged the king and his lords in the Tower of London.

14 June

Next day the king came to Mile End to meet the commons. They knelt before him and Wat Tyler said they would deal with all the traitors who were against him. Richard promised that they should have their freedom and all their wishes and that they should go through the realm and bring all the traitors to him safely to be dealt with by the law. The commons of Essex went home but Wat Tyler with some men burst in to the Tower and cut off the heads of the Archbishop of Canterbury and the Treasurer. That night they beheaded some 140 persons.

15 June

The king met the commons again. They stood in battle formation in great numbers. Tyler demanded all the lands of the Church be divided amongst the people, that all villeins should be free and there should be no lords save the king. Presently he called for a flagon of ale of which he drank a great deal.

Tyler then argued with one of the king's men and would have run him through with his dagger. Seeing this the Lord Mayor of London tried to arrest Tyler and so Wat stabbed him in the stomach. But the Mayor was wearing armour and drew his cutlass and gave Wat a great cut on the head.

When the commons saw Wat was dead they cried out to the king for mercy. The king kindly granted mercy and many of them ran away. Two knights led the rest out of London safely so they could go home.

Source K

Source L A picture from Froissart's *Chronicle* painted about 60 years after the events. It shows two scenes with Richard II. On the left he watches while Tyler is killed. On the right he speaks to the rebels.

> Their chief captain was Wat Tyler. He was a tiler of roofs and a wicked and nasty fellow he was.

Source M A noble's view of Tyler, by John Froissart

Source N An experienced soldier. From *History Makers of the Middle Ages* by Peter Crisp, 1994.

> Wat Tyler was chosen as the peasant leader. He had probably served as a soldier in France and was picked because he knew about fighting.

Remember...

- **During May to June the peasants rebelled and went to London to complain to the king.**
- **The revolt collapsed when Wat Tyler was killed.**

Investigations

1 Look at Source **I**. Why do you think the peasants were willing to trust Richard II?

2 Look at Source **J**. Why was London such an easy target for the rebels?

3 Using the evidence in Sources **K** and **L**, describe briefly what these sources tell us about:
  a) the character of Richard II
  b) the character of Wat Tyler.

4 How useful is Source **M** for anyone studying Wat Tyler? Why?

5 Is there anything in Source **K** to support the view in Source **N** that Tyler was an ex-soldier?

Were the peasants betrayed?

Once the rebels had left London, the Great Revolt was as good as over. The king gathered his armies, and judges were sent out to capture peasant ringleaders. Richard broke his promises (Source **R**), saying he only made them because he was being threatened. For a time the peasants were treated more harshly than ever.

The revolt was a failure, but some changes did happen as a result of the protest. A poll tax was never tried again until the 1980s. Gradually many lords began to realise that it was better to pay willing labourers to farm their land rather than force villeins to do work service.

Source O The king's words to Essex peasants. From Thomas Walsingham's *History of England*, 1381.

> Oh you wretched men. You who want to be equal with your lords are not worthy to live. Villeins you were and villeins you shall remain.

Source P Nobles take revenge on the peasants

Source Q Harsh use of the law. From the *Chronicle* of Henry Knighton, written in about 1381.

> Judge Tresilian spared no one. Peasants accused of rebellion, whether justly or out of hatred, were beheaded, hung or drawn and quartered. John Ball was drawn and quartered. His intestines were cut out and burned while he was still alive. Then he was hung and his body cut into four. Pieces were sent to be put on show in different places in the kingdom.

Source R The king takes pity. From *The Anonimalle Chronicle*, written about 1381.

> Finally the king saw that too much blood would be spilled. He took pity on the rebels and gave them full pardon provided they did not rise up again. Everyone was given a document showing that they had been forgiven but had to pay a fee of 20 shillings [£1] for the royal seal to make it legal.

Remember...

- **The king went back on his promises and the peasants were punished.**
- **The Great Revolt was a failure, but work service slowly ended and more people became free men.**

Investigations

1 Look at Source **O**, and Source **K** on page 36. What promise has the king broken? Do you think this was wrong of him?

2 **a)** What does Source **P** tell us about how the nobles felt after the rebellion?
b) Compare Source **P** with Source **L** on page 37. What do the peasants look like in each picture? Which is likely to be the most most accurate? Why might the artists have made the peasants look like this?

3 Read Source **Q**. Why do you think John Ball was given such a cruel death?

4 How much was the poll tax in 1380 (Source **G** on page 35)? Now read Source **R**. Is the king really taking pity on the rebels? Explain your answer.

The Wars of the Roses

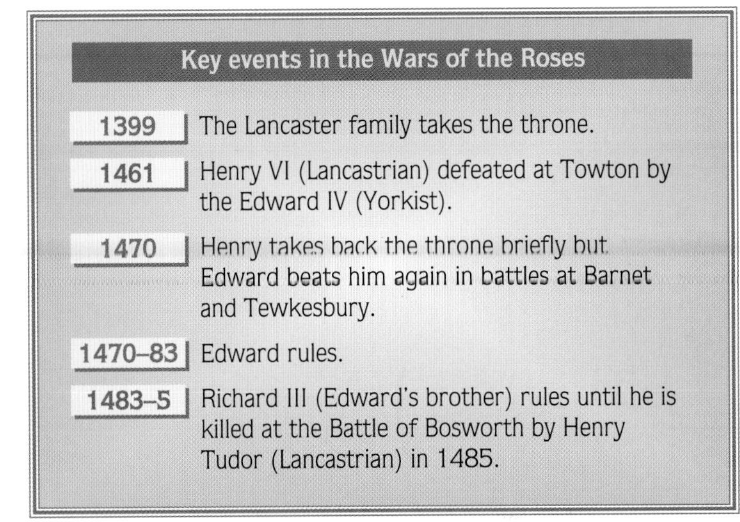

Key events in the Wars of the Roses	
1399	The Lancaster family takes the throne.
1461	Henry VI (Lancastrian) defeated at Towton by the Edward IV (Yorkist).
1470	Henry takes back the throne briefly but Edward beats him again in battles at Barnet and Tewkesbury.
1470–83	Edward rules.
1483–5	Richard III (Edward's brother) rules until he is killed at the Battle of Bosworth by Henry Tudor (Lancastrian) in 1485.

York and Lancaster

From the 1450s until 1485 England was divided by the Wars of the Roses. The fighting was between two noble families – York and Lancaster. Both families were descended from Edward III, and both believed they had the best claim to the throne. The Yorkists wore a white rose as their badge, the Lancastrians chose a red rose.

The chart on the right shows the main events in the wars.

Richard III

Richard III was an able king, but he made one big mistake. Edward IV's young sons disappeared, and Richard was suspected of ordering their murder. This split the York family, and many of them backed Henry Tudor when he invaded and challenged Richard.

Although the wars appear to have lasted over 30 years, the time spent actually fighting was only about one year. The battles were usually fought by small armies of nobles and their followers, and casualties were light. Life for most people went on as normal.

Historians often use the year 1485 to mark the end of the Middle Ages and the beginning of what is known as the Early Modern Period.

Richard II was deposed in 1399 and probably murdered in 1400 on the orders of Henry Bolingbroke, son of John of Gaunt. It was usual for the crown to be passed on from father to son or to a nearest relative. Taking the crown by force left the Lancaster family with an uncertain and tottering crown. For the next century rival families fought for the crown giving England years of civil war and misrule.

From *The Making of England* by C. Warren Hollister

Source A The Lancasters' claim to the throne

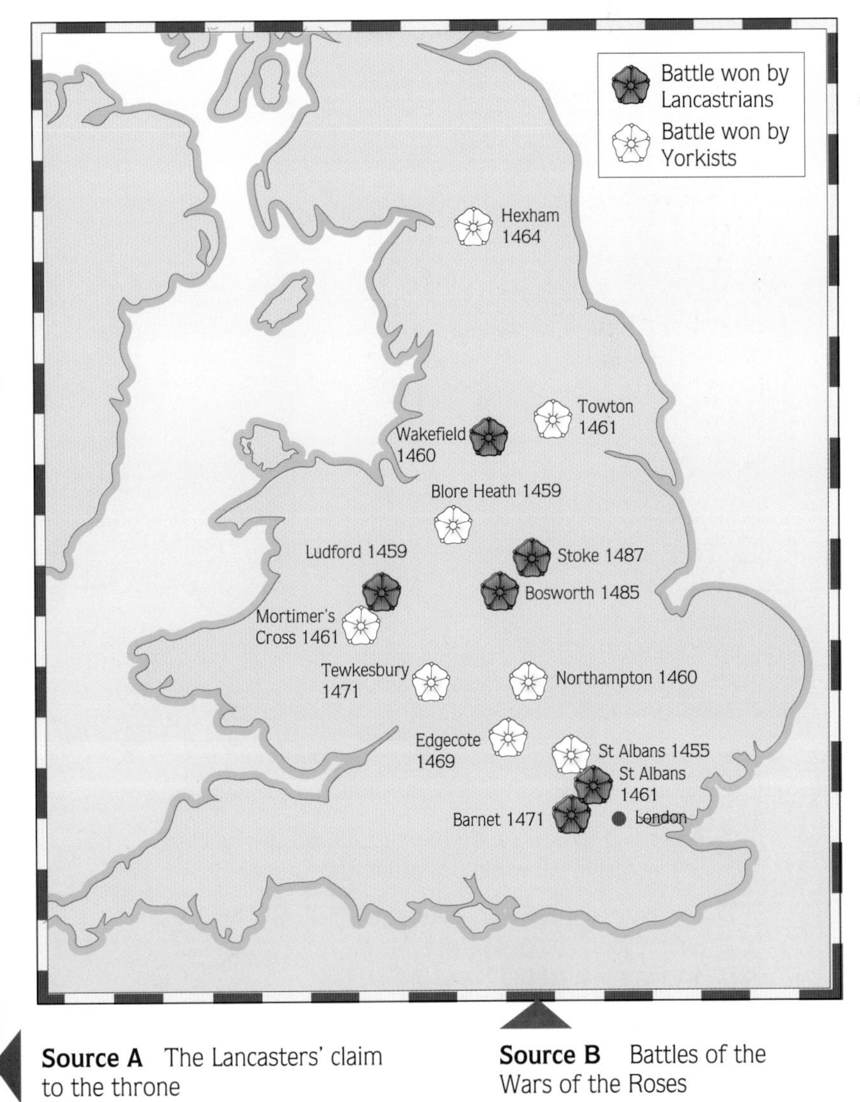

Source B Battles of the Wars of the Roses

Source C The royal family tree, from Edward III to Henry VII

Investigations

1. According to Source **A** what mistake did the Lancaster family make? How did this affect the future?
2. There were three wars between 1459 and 1487. Use Source **B** to complete these dates.
   - First War of the Roses 1459-
   - Second War of the Roses 1469-
   - Third War of the Roses 1485-
3. Using Source **C**, write two lists of the Lancastrian and Yorkist kings, showing the number of years they were each in power. Which side held the throne the longest?
4. Source **C** shows how people were related to each other. What did Henry VII do to become friends with the York family?

3 Britain and the wider world

The medieval world

How far did people travel in medieval times?

What was travel like in medieval times?

Today we can travel to the other side of the world in a matter of hours and see the world from space. In medieval times people who wanted to make journeys could travel no faster than the pace of a horse or the speed of a sailing ship. They also risked the dangers of bad weather and robbers.

Kings, soldiers, traders and pilgrims had to deal with these problems when they travelled. Most people did not venture far from the place where they lived. They would be likely to be born, live all their lives and die in the same small area.

What did a medieval map of the world look like?

It is not surprising that people's knowledge of the world was not very great. Source **A** is based on a very famous medieval map called the Mappa Mundi. This is Latin for 'Map of the World'.

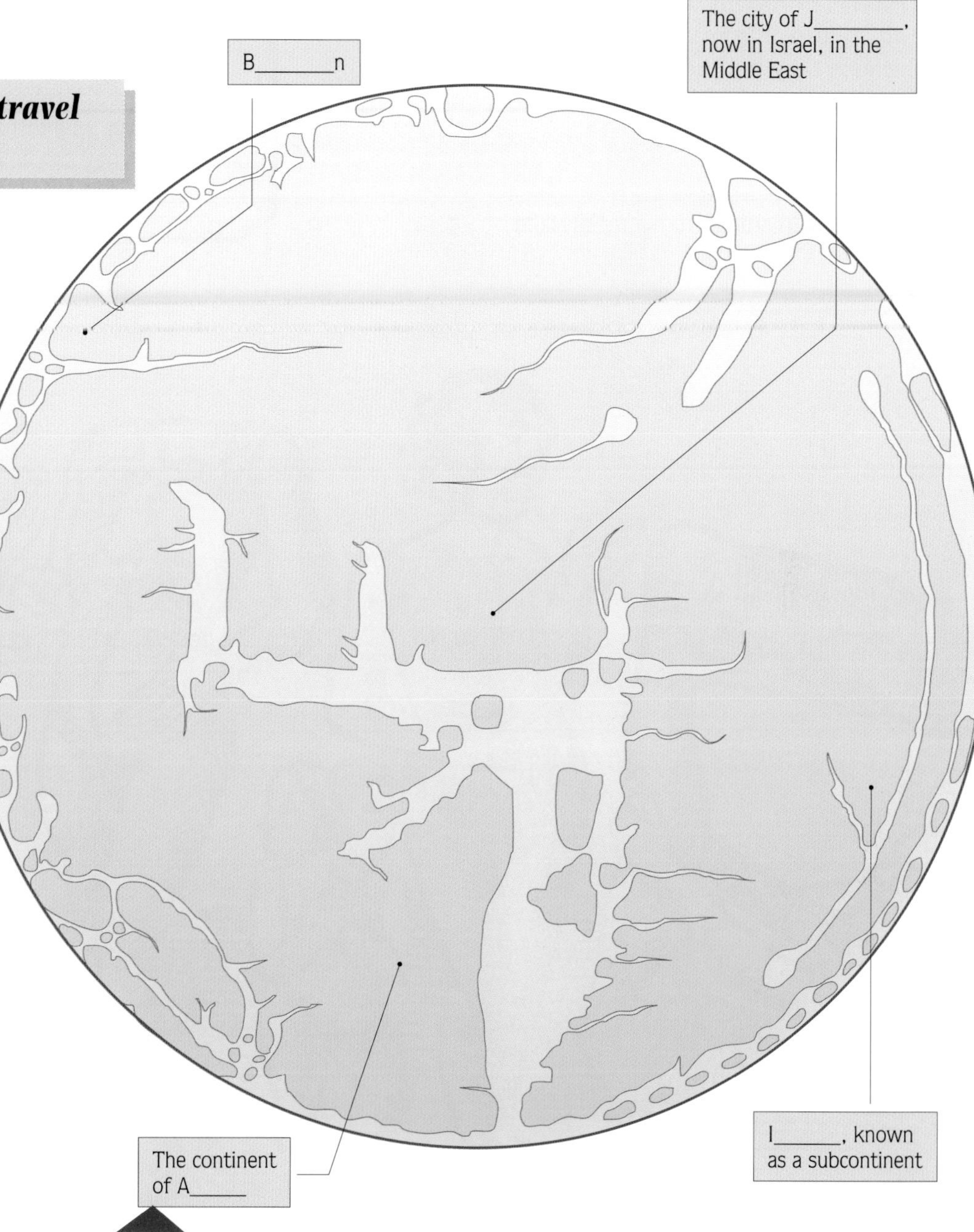

Source A This map is based on the medieval Mappa Mundi. You can see the real map for yourself if you go to Hereford Cathedral.

Investigations

1 Compare this map with a modern map of the world in an atlas.

2 a) Make a sketch of the Mappa Mundi and fill in the answers in the boxes.
b) What is the name of the city which begins with the letter 'J'? Why should this city be placed at the centre of the map? (Remember: almost everyone living in Europe at the time was a Christian.)
c) What continents and seas are missing?
d) What other things are wrong about this map compared to what we know today?

What did medieval Europeans think the world was like?

Travellers brought back information about people and creatures from other parts of the world. Because they had no cameras, travellers could only describe what they had seen in words and pictures.

Source B Sir John Mandeville wrote down a description of people living in distant places

In one of the islands in the Far East are giants horrible to look at. They have only one eye in the middle of their forehead and they eat nothing but raw flesh and fish. In another isle there are people with lips so big that they can cover their faces with them as they sleep in the sun.

Source C Creatures from a far-off land

Remember...

- **Travel was very difficult in medieval times**
- **Europeans' knowledge of the world was not very great.**

Investigations

1. **a)** Make sketches of the creatures in Sir John Mandeville's description (Source **B**).
   b) Might anything in this description be true?
2. Work in pairs. Invent a creature and write a brief description of it. Swap descriptions, and draw the creature your partner has described. Swap drawings. Has your partner drawn your creature accurately? What is different about it?
3. How might this help you to understand why medieval writers believed in fantastical creatures?

Medieval Britain

What did a map of medieval Britain look like?

As you will have seen, medieval Europeans knew very little about what the world actually looked like. They knew a little more about their own countries but, even then, there were differences.

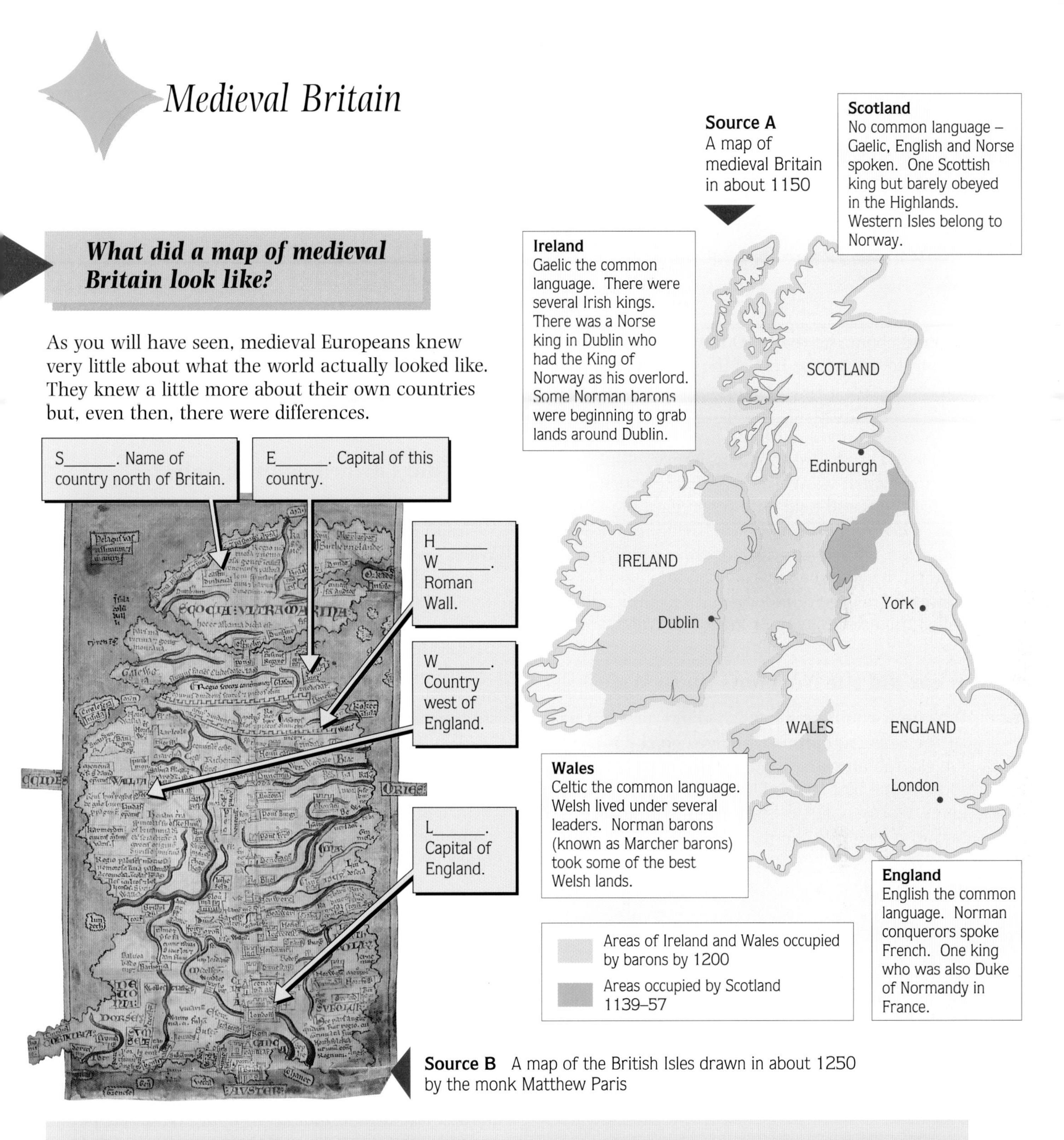

Source A A map of medieval Britain in about 1150

Source B A map of the British Isles drawn in about 1250 by the monk Matthew Paris

Investigations

1 a) Compare Matthew Paris's map (Source **B**) with a modern map of the British Isles in an atlas.
b) Make a sketch of Matthew Paris's map and fill in the boxes.
c) What has changed and what has stayed the same?
d) Which country is missing from Matthew Paris's map of the British Isles?
e) In what ways is Matthew Paris's map wrong?
f) Is the place where you live marked? If not, why might this be?

2 Compare the map in Source **A** with modern-day Britain and complete the table below.

	Medieval times	Today
Population		
Countries of the British Isles		
Capital cities		
Separate or united?		

Medieval Wales

Who were the Welsh?

Around about the year 410 the Roman legions left Britain to defend the rest of the Roman Empire in Europe. Saxon invaders poured into Britain and pushed the British westwards.

Some Britons stayed and lived alongside the invaders. Others fled to Wales, a mountainous country which was easier to defend. British tribes settled there and held onto this region of the British Isles. They remained after the Norman invasion and conquest. The Welsh word for their country is 'Cymru' which means 'people of one region'. However, they lived under several leaders and none called themselves King or Prince of Wales.

What did the Normans do to Wales?

William was not very interested in Wales but he did let the Norman barons who lived on the border with Wales grab any land they could. They captured some of the best Welsh farmland in the lowland areas. Norman castles sprang up to guard what they had won from the Welsh.

The Welsh fight back

From about 1160 the Welsh began to fight back. They took advantage of the quarrels in England between the king and his barons and the wars with France. The Welsh princes banded together and began to win back land from the English. In 1267, the Welsh prince of Gwynedd won the title of 'Prince of Wales' from the English king whom he had defeated.

How did England conquer Wales?

In 1272 Edward I became King of England. He was determined to make Wales part of his kingdom. Llywelyn, the most powerful prince in Wales, refused to accept the English king as **overlord**, so Edward led an English army into Wales and surrounded Llywelyn near Snowdonia. Starving, Llywelyn finally had to give in.

Despite defeat, Llywelyn was soon back in action. But the revolt did not last long. Llywelyn was killed in battle and his head stuck on a spear on top of the Tower of London.

How did Edward control Wales?

Edward now had to make sure he could hold onto Wales in case the Welsh found another 'Prince of Wales' to follow. Huge castles were built all over Wales – the strongest was in Gwynedd where the most trouble had occurred. The total cost of building the castles was huge for the times – £100,000.

Edward also encouraged English people to move into Wales and settle there. In this way he might be sure of people who were loyal to him.

Whilst Edward was in Wales his wife, Eleanor, gave birth to their son. Edward hit upon a powerful idea. When his son was 16 he gave him the title of 'Prince of Wales' so that no Welsh prince could claim the title for himself. Ever since that time, the English ruler's eldest son has been given the title.

Why did the Welsh rebel again?

Wales remained more or less peaceful, but beneath the surface many Welsh people still hated being ruled by the English. In 1400, a young Welsh knight called Owen Glyn Dwr (the last two parts to his name are said as 'Glendowwer') led a rebellion against the English. He fought them for fifteen years and eventually became an outlaw. He refused a free pardon and died in hiding. To many Welsh people today he remains a hero of their country's wish to be independent from England.

Key words

Overlord A lord who is above other lords.
Scourge Cause of suffering.
Trojans The heroes of Troy were believed to be the ancestors of the Welsh.

Source A Map of Wales showing the rise of Llywelyn and the castles of Edward I

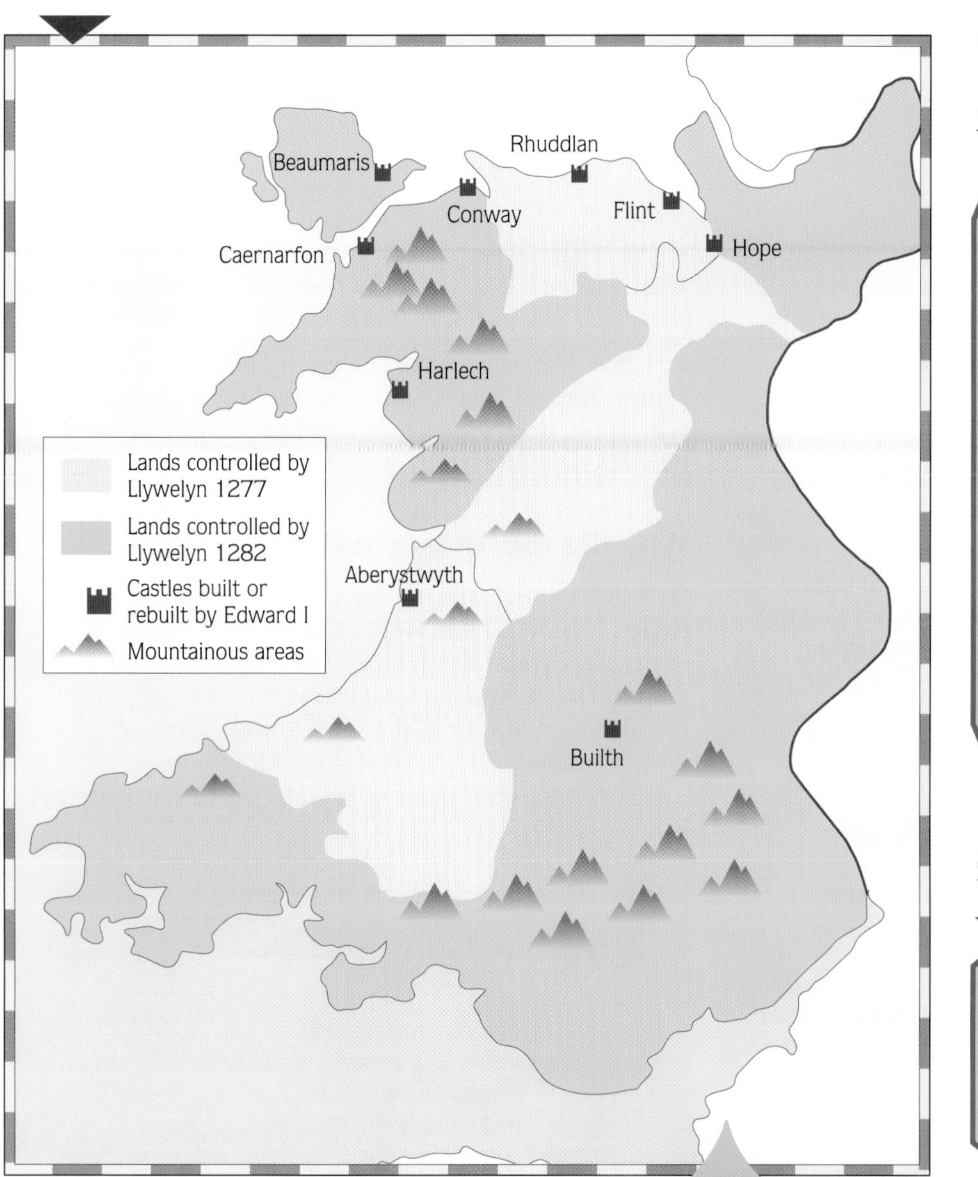

Source B These are two poems about Llywelyn. One was written by a Welsh monk and the other by an English monk. They were collected by William Risingham in the thirteenth century in *Chronicles and Annals*.

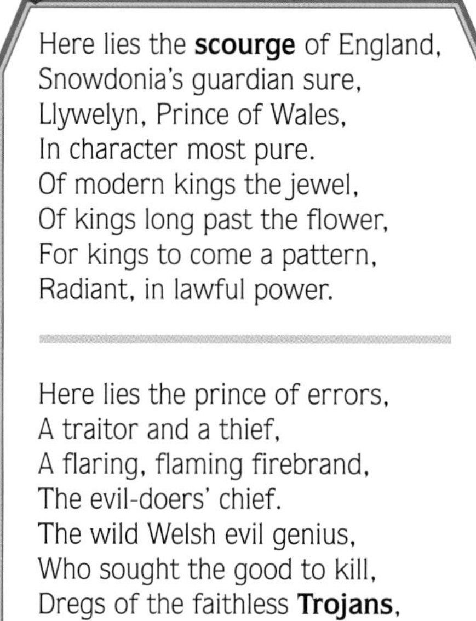

Here lies the **scourge** of England,
Snowdonia's guardian sure,
Llywelyn, Prince of Wales,
In character most pure.
Of modern kings the jewel,
Of kings long past the flower,
For kings to come a pattern,
Radiant, in lawful power.

Here lies the prince of errors,
A traitor and a thief,
A flaring, flaming firebrand,
The evil-doers' chief.
The wild Welsh evil genius,
Who sought the good to kill,
Dregs of the faithless **Trojans**,
And source of every evil.

Source C From the *Chronicle* of Gerald of Wales, a Welsh monk, written in 1250

The Welsh people are fierce rather than strong. They are all trained in war. They love freedom and are determined to defend their country.

Source D From the *Chronicle* of Roger of Wendover, an English monk, written in 1231

In May the Welsh burst forth from their dens like shrews from holes, raising fires everywhere. They spared neither churches nor priests and those noble women and girls who had sought safety were burned along with the churches themselves.

Remember...

- **Many of the Welsh were the ancestors of the Britons who had been pushed westward by Saxon invaders.**
- **Welsh princes tried to keep parts of Wales independent but the country was conquered by the English king, Edward I.**

Investigations

1 Look at the map in Source **A**. What sort of country is Wales? Would it be easy for an army to fight there? With your partner, decide the best plan of attack. You can attack from several different directions, but remember:
- The more you split your army up the weaker it becomes.
- A large army will need supplies. It is easiest to send these by sea. If on land you will need to follow the main valleys.

2 Read Source **B**.
a) Which poem was written by the English monk and which by the Welsh monk?
b) What sort of words do the monks use to describe Llywelyn?
c) Why are these sources biased?

3 Read Sources **C** and **D**.
a) Do they give very different descriptions of the Welsh?
b) Which do you think is more likely to be true? Why?

Medieval Scotland

How did Scotland remain independent of England?

What was medieval Scotland like?

Scotland is a land divided in two. To the north there are mountains and lakes in an area we now call the Highlands. In medieval times, Highlanders spoke a different language, called Gaelic. They lived in tribes, called clans.

Further south are lower-lying lands which are better for farming. Here, in the Lowlands, Norman barons claimed land and built castles. Norman monks built monasteries. Most Scottish people in the Lowlands spoke English.

Despite the two different parts of Scotland, Scottish people wanted to remain seperate from England.

Why did England want to control Scotland?

England was often at war with France during medieval times. Scotland was friendly with France, and so the English were afraid that they might be attacked from two directions.

In 1072 William had marched an army through Scotland as a show of strength. After that, English kings always claimed they were Scotland's overlord, but the Scots remained independent.

In 1286 there was a crisis in Scotland. Alexander III of Scotland was killed, leaving no obvious person to become their ruler, so the Scots asked Edward I of England to decide on a new king. He agreed to do so, as long as the Scots accepted him as their overlord. The Scottish Parliament reluctantly agreed.

Who did Edward choose?

The man Edward chose was John Baliol, an important landowner. As soon as Baliol became king, he rejected Edward as overlord. Edward's soldiers marched into Scotland, got rid of Baliol and conquered the country.

The Scots soon rose in rebellion against Edward led by a knight called William Wallace. A year later, in 1298, the Scots were beaten at Falkirk, and a traitor handed over Wallace to the English. Wallace was hung, drawn and quartered and the remains of his body put on display in towns all over England.

Why did the Scots continue to fight?

Soon after the death of Edward I in 1307, the Scots rallied behind a new leader, Robert Bruce. Edward II of England could not ignore this challenge to England's overlordship. After several attempts, he invaded Scotland in 1314 with a huge army of 20 000 men.

They met on a piece of marshy ground called Bannockburn.

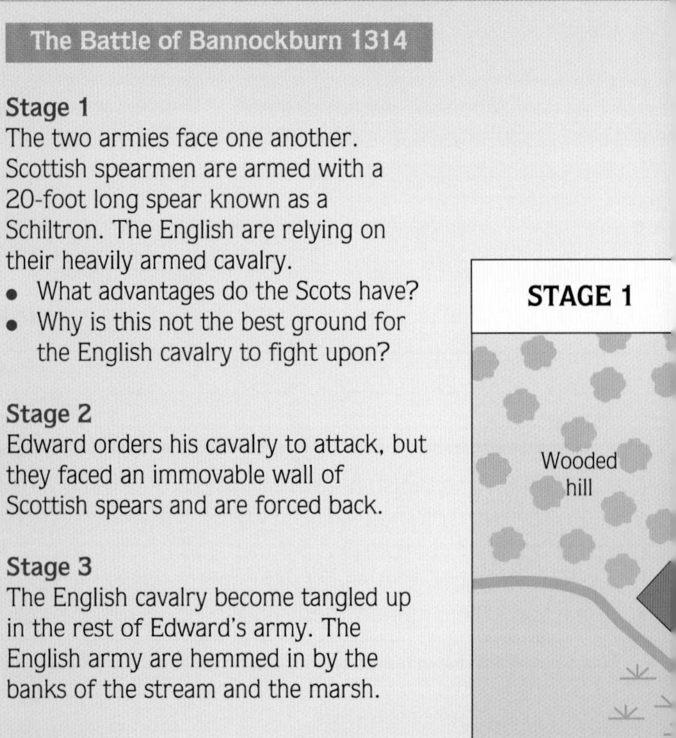

The Battle of Bannockburn 1314

Stage 1
The two armies face one another. Scottish spearmen are armed with a 20-foot long spear known as a Schiltron. The English are relying on their heavily armed cavalry.

- What advantages do the Scots have?
- Why is this not the best ground for the English cavalry to fight upon?

Stage 2
Edward orders his cavalry to attack, but they faced an immovable wall of Scottish spears and are forced back.

Stage 3
The English cavalry become tangled up in the rest of Edward's army. The English army are hemmed in by the banks of the stream and the marsh.

Stage 4
The Scots army move in and slaughter the English army who cannot escape. A few hours later the tide comes in and drowns the wounded and the dying.

Bannockburn was a defeat from which the English never recovered. At the Treaty of Northampton in 1328, Edward III agreed that Scotland was an independent country separate from England. Border warfare continued between the two countries, and Scotland nearly always took advantage to invade England when the English army was away fighting in France. The situation remained the same until 1603, when the King of Scotland, James VI, inherited the crown of England and became James I.

Source A From the *Chronicle* of Henry of Huntingdon, 1138

King David of Scotland encouraged his followers to deal most cruelly with the English. They ripped open pregnant women and pulled out unborn babies; they tossed the children on the points of their spears and butchered priests at the altar. Therefore King Stephen of England invaded Scotland.

Source B
From *The Deeds of Stephen* by an anonymous writer

The King of Scotland, David, was a kind and caring prince who was born of religious parents. The natives of Scotland are savage. Swift of foot and lightly armed they make bold and active soldiers. Towards strangers they are cruel and brutal.

Source C From the *Chronicle* of Walter of Guisborough

Edward I, King of England, sent letters to John Baliol, King of Scotland, asking him for some of his finest soldiers to fight against France. But the Scots, having made a treaty of friendship with Philip IV, King of France, refused.

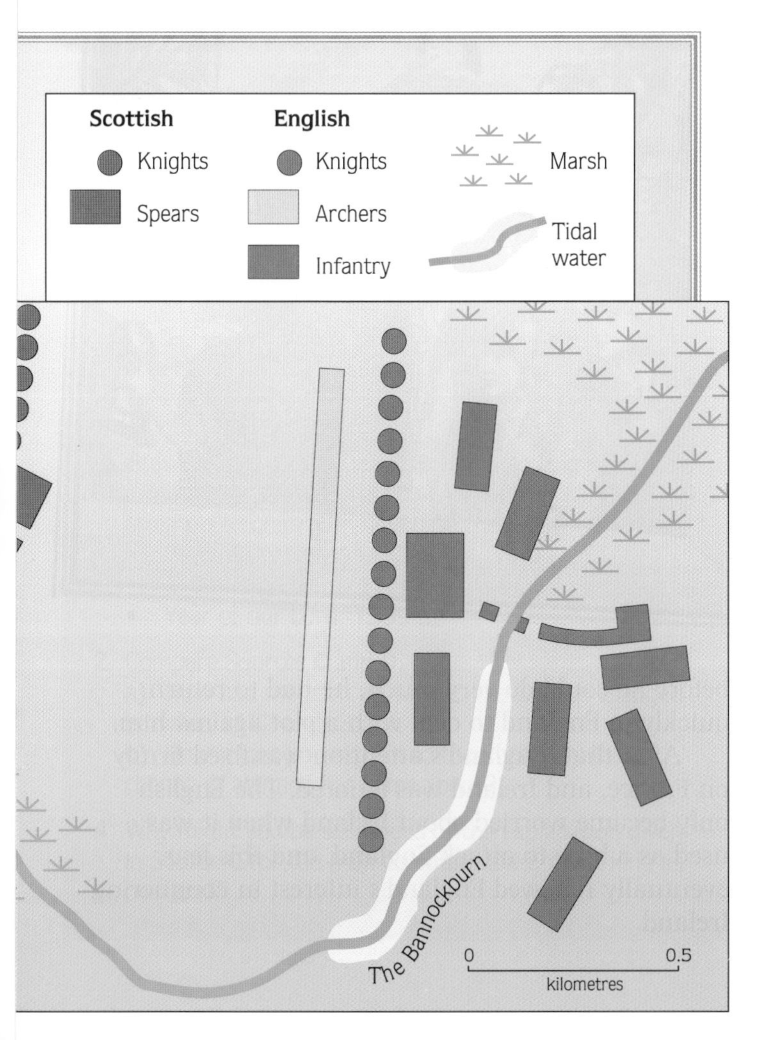

Remember...

- **From the time of William the Conqueror English kings had claimed they were the overlords of Scotland. England invaded the country several times to prove this claim.**
- **The Scots were able to remain independent throughout medieval times by defeating Edward II at the Battle of Bannockburn.**

Investigations

1. In pairs, each draw a timeline to describe the main events which led to the Battle of Bannockburn. One person should present the events from the Scottish point of view, the other from the English point of view.
   - If both timelines use the same events, how and why are they different?
2. Read Sources **A** and **B** carefully.
   a) What do these sources say about King David?
   b) What do they say about the Scots?
   c) What are the differences in each case?
   d) Why might the sources say different things?
3. Read Source **C** carefully. The Scots had accepted the English kings as their overlords. But the Scots explained they had a treaty of friendship with France.
   a) As an English lawyer explain why they should have obeyed Edward.
   b) As a Scottish lawyer explain why they could not obey Edward in this case.
4. Copy the plan of Stage 1 of the Battle of Bannockburn. Use this to help you draw plans of Stages 2–4, based on the written descriptions.

England and France

- ***Why were England and France enemies?***
- ***What was the Hundred Years War?***

In 1066 England had been invaded and conquered from France by William the Conqueror. For the next five hundred years Britain and France squabbled and fought for possession of the French kingdom.

The fighting did not go on all the time. Sometimes the two countries settled their differences in a peace treaty and there were long periods of peace, but sooner or later a quarrel would occur and the two armies would clash. All of the fighting took place in France.

What was the cause of the fighting between England and France?

Every English king between 1199 and 1461 married a French princess or noblewoman. You might think this would have brought peace between the countries. It was usual for countries to become **allies** through marriage connections. In this case, however, it caused many of the complications which led to war.

Through marriage, the English kings acquired more and more land in France. During the reign of King Henry II (1154–1189), for example, he ruled a vast empire stretching from Scotland to Spain. Henry ruled more of France than the French king himself. Furthermore, French nobles played one king off against the other so that they could remain powerful themselves. The most troublesome French nobles were the Dukes of Burgundy. They ruled land to the north and west of France, and thought of themselves as independent of the French king.

What was the problem?

The French argued that the English lands in France were part of the realm of France and therefore the English king should do **homage** to the French king for them. The English kings disagreed and argued that they had inherited the lands through marriage and therefore they had the right to rule them.

In the end the problem solved itself. During the reign of one of Henry's sons, King John (1199–1216), all of these lands, apart from Gascony and Calais, were won back by the French.

What were the causes of the Hundred Years War?

Edward III's claim to the French throne was one important cause of the outbreak of war. However, with any important event there is usually more than one cause, and some are more important than others. It is important to understand this, because the fighting that broke out in 1337 was to last on and off for over one hundred years. For these wars to be called 'The Hundred Years War' there must have been some very deep causes to the quarrel.

Causes of the Hundred Years War

- Edward III enjoyed warfare and wanted glory and excitement.
- The French king threatened to take over Gascony. This part of France supplied England with most of its wine. The English king received **revenue** from the import of this wine. Kings were always short of money particularly when they had to fight wars and had to pay for armies.
- The French threatened England's wool trade with Flanders. This was England's most important export trade. If the trade was stopped then this would make England poorer. People would pay less in taxes to the king.
- Edward III was trying to conquer Scotland. The French promised to help the Scots.
- Edward held lands in France. He was meant to do homage to the French king for these lands. This meant that the French king could call on the English king to fight for him in war.
- The French king, Philip IV, took over Acquitaine, an area under the control of the English king.
- Edward III was the grandson of Philip IV of France. He claimed he had more right to be King of France than Philip VI.

Source A The French and English royal families

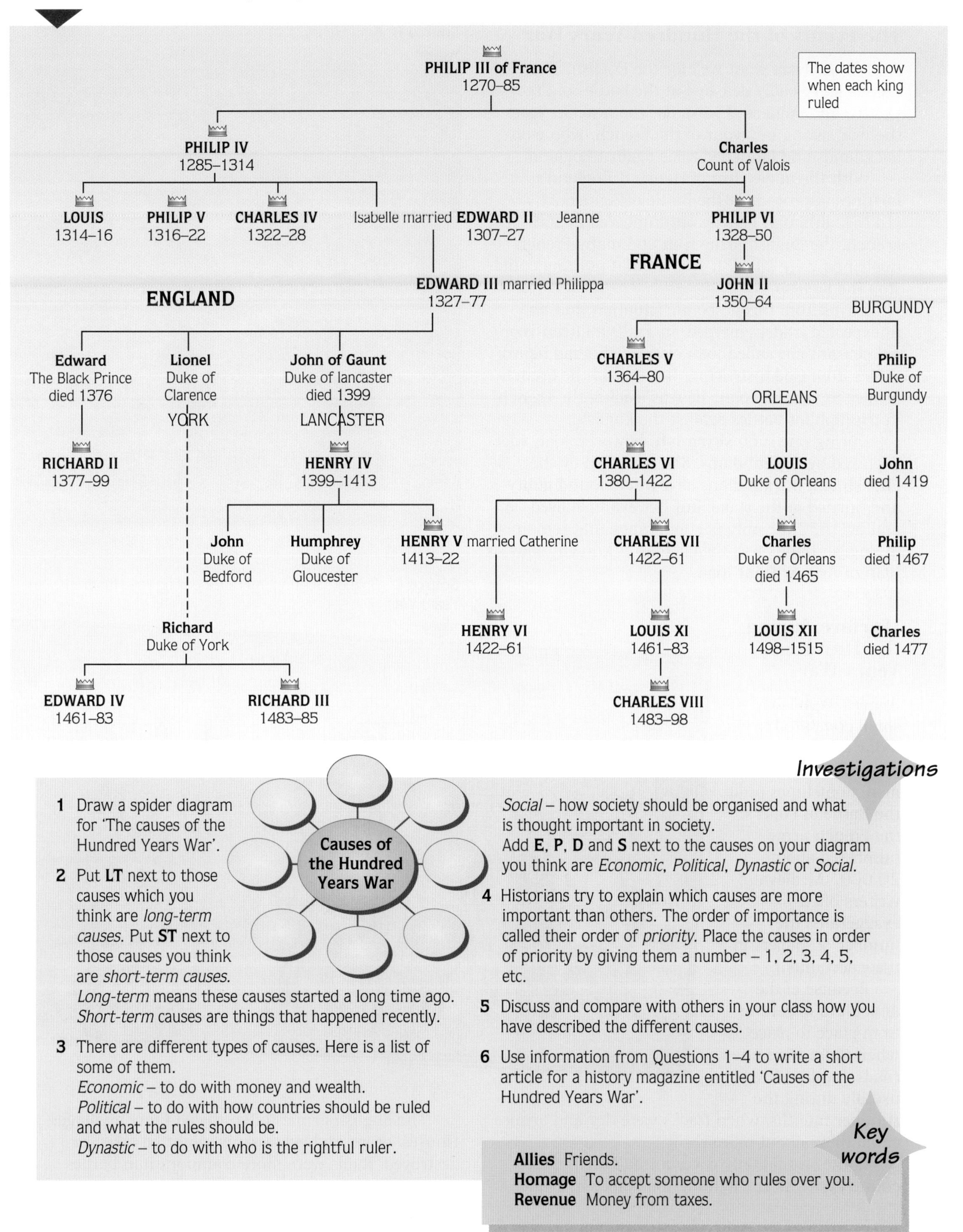

Investigations

1. Draw a spider diagram for 'The causes of the Hundred Years War'.
2. Put **LT** next to those causes which you think are *long-term causes*. Put **ST** next to those causes you think are *short-term causes*.
   Long-term means these causes started a long time ago. *Short-term* causes are things that happened recently.
3. There are different types of causes. Here is a list of some of them.
   Economic – to do with money and wealth.
   Political – to do with how countries should be ruled and what the rules should be.
   Dynastic – to do with who is the rightful ruler.
   Social – how society should be organised and what is thought important in society.
   Add **E**, **P**, **D** and **S** next to the causes on your diagram you think are *Economic*, *Political*, *Dynastic* or *Social*.
4. Historians try to explain which causes are more important than others. The order of importance is called their order of *priority*. Place the causes in order of priority by giving them a number – 1, 2, 3, 4, 5, etc.
5. Discuss and compare with others in your class how you have described the different causes.
6. Use information from Questions 1–4 to write a short article for a history magazine entitled 'Causes of the Hundred Years War'.

Key words

Allies Friends.
Homage To accept someone who rules over you.
Revenue Money from taxes.

The events of the Hundred Years War

At first the wars went well for the English. The French were badly defeated at the battles of Crecy (1346) and Poitiers (1356). For the next 50 years the war swung in favour of the French, who won back lands and launched raids against England.

With the **accession** of Henry V, England's fortunes improved. At the Battle of Agincourt (1415), although heavily outnumbered by the French, the English army won and many French noblemen were killed. It seemed that nothing could stop the English.

It was from this desperate situation that an unexpected leader emerged. In 1429 a fifteen-year-old peasant girl called Joan claimed she had heard voices from God instructing her to lead the French armies to victory. Soon she was leading the French in triumphant battles against the English.

During one such **skirmish**, however, Joan was captured by Burgundians. She was tried by the English and Burgundians as a witch, found guilty and burned at the stake. But her example lived on, and by 1453 the only part of France that remained in English hands was Calais. Joan is known today as Joan of Arc, or Saint Joan.

Source B King Henry V

Warfare during the Hundred Years War

Armies were fairly small compared to today – usually about 5–10 000 men. Sometimes as at the Battle of Poiters, the French army numbered about 20 000. (Medieval writers often exaggerated the number of soldiers in their accounts.)

Because of the difficulties of getting from place to place when there were no roads, battles were usually during the summer months, when tracks were dry and armies could move about more easily.

Battles would only cover a small area of the countryside. All the fighting took place in France.

Source C Soldiers looting in France during the Hundred Years War

The English armies often raided French villages. Houses, crops and possessions might be taken or destroyed. Raids were more common than battles (Source **C**).

What were the effects of the Hundred Years War?

Source D English territory in France 1150–1450

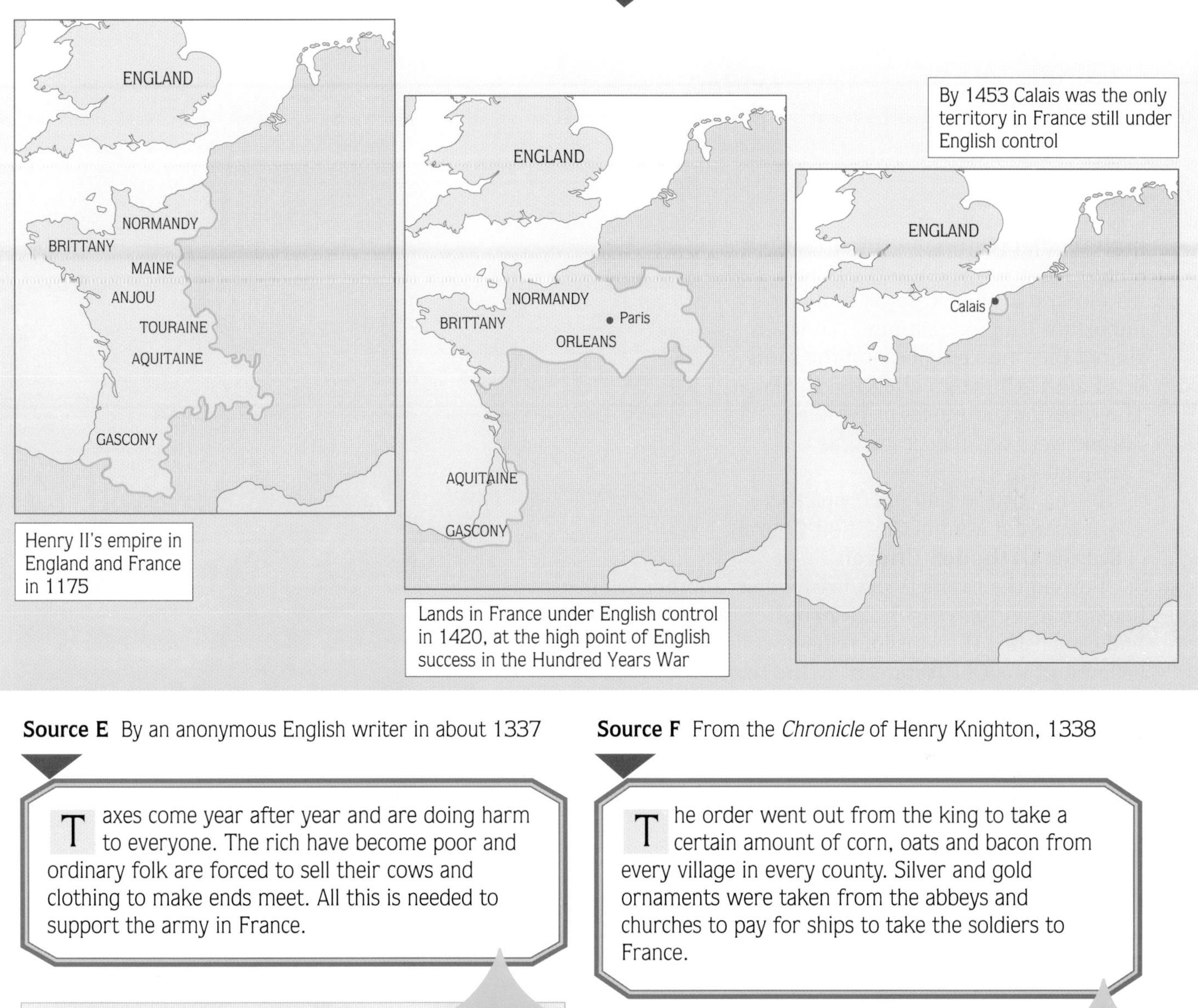

Henry II's empire in England and France in 1175

Lands in France under English control in 1420, at the high point of English success in the Hundred Years War

By 1453 Calais was the only territory in France still under English control

Source E By an anonymous English writer in about 1337

Taxes come year after year and are doing harm to everyone. The rich have become poor and ordinary folk are forced to sell their cows and clothing to make ends meet. All this is needed to support the army in France.

Source F From the *Chronicle* of Henry Knighton, 1338

The order went out from the king to take a certain amount of corn, oats and bacon from every village in every county. Silver and gold ornaments were taken from the abbeys and churches to pay for ships to take the soldiers to France.

Remember...

- **England and France frequently fought against one another throughout medieval times.**
- **The English kings claimed to be the rightful rulers of parts of France.**
- **The wars between England and France are known as The Hundred Years War.**
- **By 1453 only Calais was left under English control.**

Key words

Accession When a king or queen comes to the throne.
Skirmish A small battle.

Investigations

1. Use the information on these pages to make a list of the effects of the Hundred Years War on both England and France.
2. How badly do you think England was affected in the following ways?
   - Destruction of property
   - Wealth of the country (was England better or worse off because of the wars?)
   - Political effects (think about the victories and the defeats)
   - Loss of territory in France
3. Who do you think was worse affected by the wars – England or France? Give reasons for your answer.

Depth Study: The Crusades

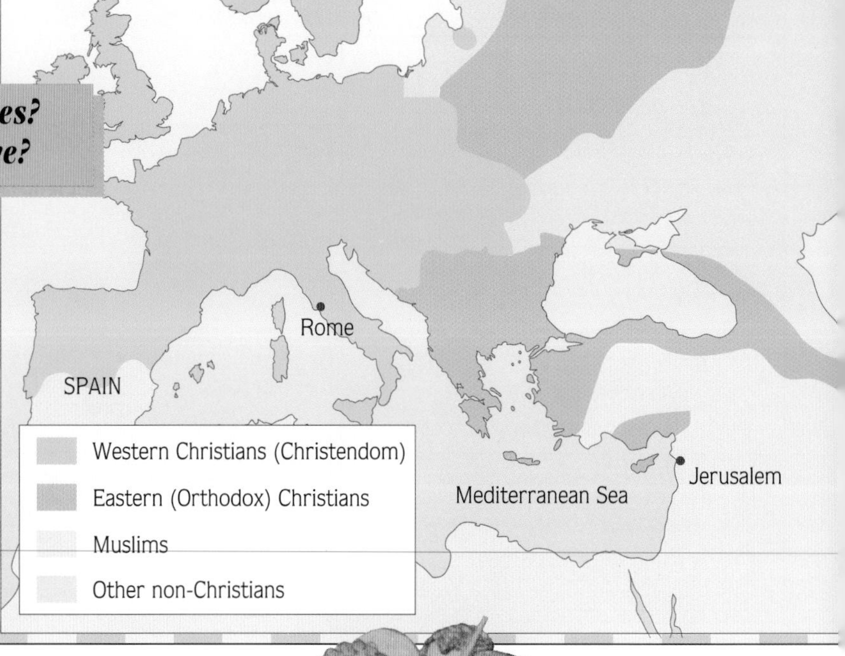

Source A Map of Christendom and the Muslim world in medieval times

- ***Why did people go on Crusades?***
- ***What did the Crusades achieve?***

Christendom

Even though many countries in Europe fought against one another, such as Britain and France, they all had one important thing in common. They all shared the same religion and the same head of the Christian church – the Pope. The Christian countries of Western Europe were together known as Christendom.

In the eastern half of Europe there was a different kind of Christian Church, called the **Orthodox Church**.

Beyond the frontiers of Christendom another religion had taken root. In the year 622 a **prophet** called **Muhammad** had established the Muslim religion called Islam. Muslims believed in the Old Testament of the Bible, as Christians did, but not the New Testament. They had their own beliefs recorded in a book called the **Qur'an**.

Muslim armies had conquered lands around the Mediterranean Sea, and ruled over part of Spain.

Source B Medieval pilgrims

Jerusalem

Pilgrims travelled all over Europe to visit holy places. They believed making such journeys would please God. The holiest place to visit was Jerusalem where Jesus had been crucified. The Muslims also thought of Jerusalem as a holy city.

Key words

Orthodox Church The Christian Church in Eastern Europe.
Muhammad Founder of the Muslim religion.
Prophet A person sent to tell God's message.
Qur'an The holy book of the Muslim religion.

Remember...

- **All the people of Western Europe belonged to the Christian Church, headed by the Pope. This was called Christendom.**
- **Beyond Christendom lay the territories of the Muslim religion, Islam.**

Investigations

1 Look at Source **A**.
   a) Find out the names of those countries that were part of the medieval Muslim world.
   b) Find out if Islam is still important in these countries today.
   c) What does this tell you about the strength of Muslim belief?

2 **a)** Collect pictures to do with Islam.
   b) Find out five facts about Islam.

3 Jerusalem was thought to be very holy by Christians and Muslims.
   a) Was Jerusalem in Christian or Muslim territory?
   b) What difficulties might this have made for Christian pilgrims?

Who went to fight the Crusades?

We have already seen that Jerusalem was in the hands of Muslims. On 27 November 1095 the Pope, Urban II, preached a sermon (Sources **C** and **D**). What he said made kings, knights, soldiers and even an army of children leave Europe and fight to win back Jerusalem for Christendom. What could have made them do this?

Those who did go to the Holy Land became known as Crusaders – men and women who went on a fighting pilgrimage.

Source C This is part of the sermon spoken by Urban II. It was written down by a priest called Fulcher, from Chartres in France.

> Beloved brothers, I speak as a messenger to reveal to you God's will. We cannot refuse at once to give help to our brothers in the East. They now need it desperately. The Turks and Arabs have advanced into Rumania. They have beaten the Christians seven times in a battle, have killed and captured a large number of them, have wrecked their churches and destroyed their land. If we do not go to help, the true servants of God in the East will not be able to survive.
>
> I therefore urge and beg you who are the voices of Christ, both rich and poor, to drive the foul vermin from the lands where your Christian brothers live and to bring speedy help to the worshippers of Christ. Promise your support without delay. Let the warriors get ready and find what they need to pay for the journey. When the spring comes let them leave in good spirit under the banner of the Lord.

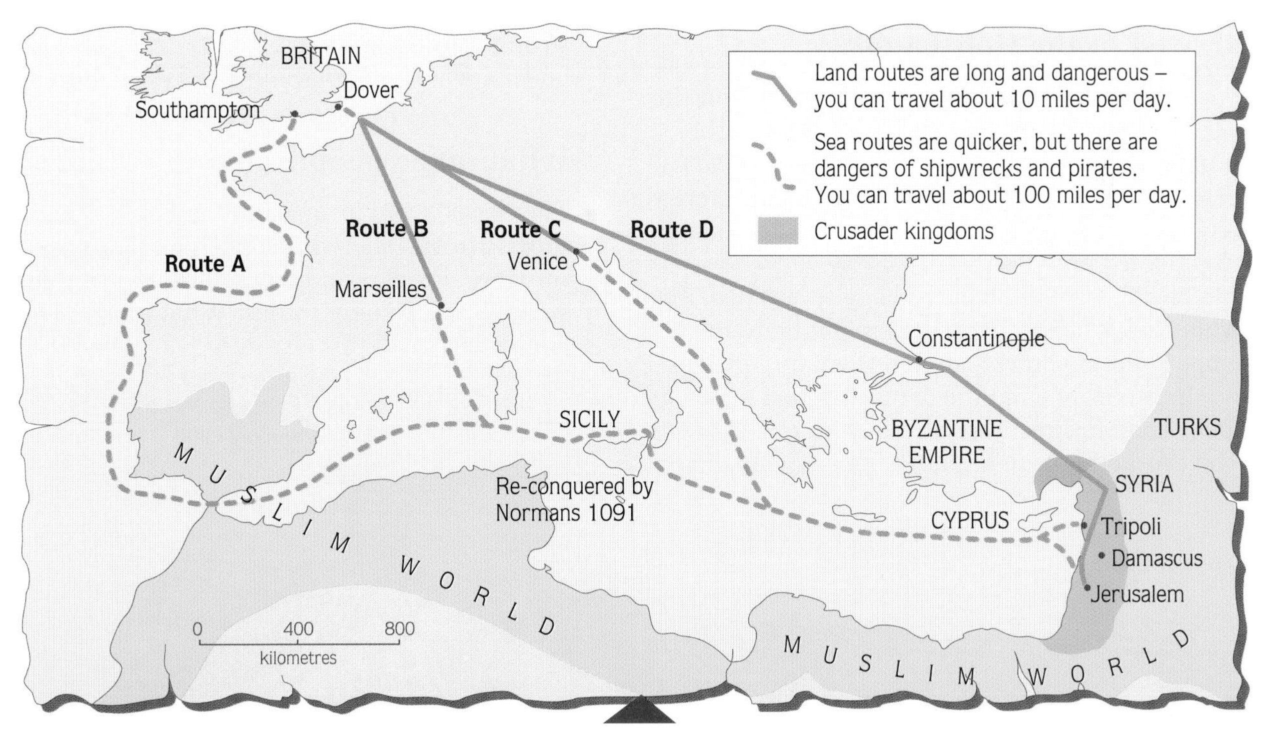

Source E Map showing routes from Europe to the Holy Land

Source D Pope Urban II preaching about the Crusades

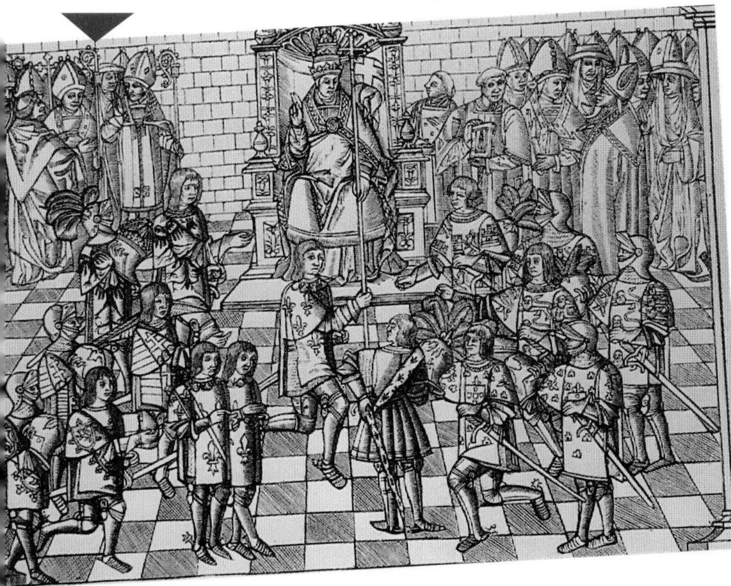

Investigations

1. Draw a recruiting poster titled 'Christendom Needs You!' What sort of illustration will you put on the poster? Which words of Urban II will you quote?
2. You are an English Crusader about to set out for the Holy Land. You can choose one of four possible routes – A, B, C or D – as shown on the map in Source **E**.
   a) What are the advantages and disadvantages of each route?
   b) Approximately how long will each route be? (Work this out using the scale on the map.)
   c) Which route would take the longest?
   d) Which route would you choose? Give your reasons.

Why did the Pope call for a Crusade?

Jerusalem had been under Muslim control for four hundred years before Pope Urban II preached his sermon. Why then did people in the west wait so long to win back the Holy Lands from Muslim control?

Although the Muslims had conquered most of the Middle East, they had failed to get any further west because the **Byzantine Empire** stood in their way. But in 1071 the Byzantine armies had suffered a massive defeat at the Battle of Manzikurt. Afraid that his empire would collapse, the Byzantine Emperor, Alexius Commenius, asked the Pope for help.

What happened when the Crusaders arrived in the Holy Land?

Pope Urban had no plan to send armies from the west to **Byzantium** and was astounded at the numbers that volunteered. Several armies of Crusaders set off for the Holy Land. There were soon reports of ugly incidents along the route. Villages were looted and destroyed.

The Emperor Alexius became so worried about what the armies of Crusaders might do to his empire that he quickly moved them on into Turkey.

In the Holy Land the Crusaders had amazing luck. The Muslims were at war with one another. The crusading armies quickly took advantage of the situation and conquered the Holy Lands, including the main prize – the holy city of Jerusalem (Source **K**).

How advanced was Muslim civilisation compared to the west?

The Crusaders set up Christian kingdoms in the lands they had conquered. Parts of these kingdoms lasted for almost two hundred years. Many Crusaders were amazed at the luxuries they found – carpets, furniture, porcelain, and new foods such as apricots and lemons.

More importantly, they recognised that Muslims were more advanced with ideas about medicine. In engineering, the Muslims were skilled at making arches and pillars which carried great weights, and strong round towers in castles and forts. They were far in advance of anything the west had to offer.

What made people go on Crusades?

The reasons why people do things is called **motivation**. Different people have different **motives**. People can have several motives at the same time for doing things. What motives can you find as you read this chapter?

Source F Crusaders loading their ship to sail to the Holy Land

What happened to the Crusaders?

Between 1096 and 1270 there were seven different Crusades to the Holy Land, but none of them repeated the success of the first. Terrible violence was committed by both sides as the hatred deepened. In times of peace, however, Muslims and Christians lived alongside one another (Source **G**).

Source G Fulcher of Chartres, a French monk. He went on the First Crusade and lived for a while in the kingdom of Jerusalem.

> We who were once Westerners are now Easterners. Many of us have our own homes, some have taken a local wife or even converted a **Saracen** and live together. He who was once a stranger is now a native.

Source H From the *Gesta Francorum* – a medieval manuscript which describes the capture of Jerusalem

> Our men entered the city and killed the unbelievers so that blood was streaming everywhere. No one was spared – women and children were put to the sword. Our men rushed round the city seizing gold and silver, horses and all sorts of goods.

Source I Pope Urban's speech as written down by William of Malmsbury

> If you take the right path, you will be forgiven all your sins. This path is to make war on the **infidels**.

In 1144 the city of Edessa was recaptured by the Muslims. The Second Crusade tried to get it back, but failed. Then, in 1187, a new Muslim leader, Saladin, attacked the Christian kingdoms and defeated the Crusaders at the Battle of Hattin. This new danger spurred the Western European kingdoms to come to the rescue.

Led by kings, who included Richard the Lionheart, the Crusaders fought several fierce battles, but failed to re-take Jerusalem.

Eventually, peace was made with Saladin, and the Crusaders sailed home again.

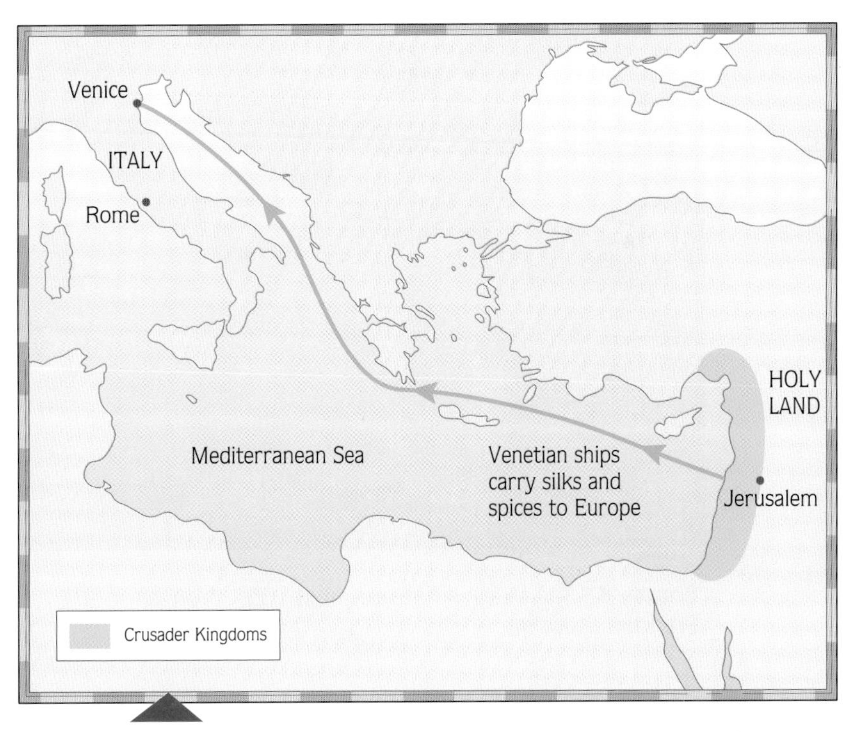

Source J Trade route to Venice from the Holy Land

Key words

Byzantine Empire The remains of the ancient Roman Empire in the east.
Byzantium The capital city of Turkey, now known as Istanbul.
Infidels Unbelievers.
Motivation/motives The reasons for doing things.
Saracen A Muslim enemy of the Crusaders.

Investigations

1. Look at Sources **H**, **I** and **J**, and identify the motives or reasons why people went on the Crusades. Present your answer as a spider diagram.
2. What motives might the following people have had for going on a crusade?

   Soldier | Pilgrim | Nobleman | Trader

3. Why do you think the Crusaders showed no mercy to women and children (Source **H**)? (Source **I** gives a clue.)
4. Why, after some time had passed, might Muslims and Christians get on well together (Source **G**)?

Source K The attack on Jerusalem in 1099, from a French manuscript

The outcome of the Crusades

Over the next one hundred years Jerusalem changed hands, but by 1291 the last of the Christian cities, Acre, fell to the Muslims. Despite the shedding of so much blood, the Crusades had failed.

Remember...

- **The purpose of the Crusades was to win back the Holy Land from the Muslims.**
- **The first Crusade was successful, and Christian kingdoms were set up in the Holy Land.**
- **A great Muslim leader, Saladin, fought back and by 1291 the Christian kingdoms were destroyed.**

Investigations

1 When a Crusader returned home, how do you think he might have described Muslim civilisation?

2 Look carefully at the picture in Source **K**.
a) What are the attackers doing when they are in the city of Jerusalem?
b) What are they doing to the inhabitants?
c) What impression does this give of Crusaders and their motives?

3 Source **K** was not painted until the fourteenth century. It shows the attack on Jerusalem in 1099. Does this mean it might not be useful to the historian? Why?

4 Look at the following statements **A–E**, and then use them to write a few paragraphs headed 'Were the Crusades successful?'
A The Crusades were launched to save Eastern Christendom.
B The Pope grew stronger because of the Crusades.
C In warfare the West gained a lot of knowledge about castle building.
D Trade between East and West was improved.
E Troublesome nobles left Europe, which made it more peaceful in the Western European kingdoms.

4 Everyday life

The village

What was life like in a medieval village?

Most people live in towns today. In medieval times most people lived in small villages. Although towns grew bigger, and there were more of them, most people still lived and worked in villages at the end of the medieval period.

Many villages became deserted as people moved away to other villages or to towns. Those villages that remained became much larger.

Source A This is a photograph taken from the air. It shows the remains of the village of Middle Ditchford in Gloucestershire. Can you tell where the fields and the buildings would have been?

How do we know what life was like in a medieval village?

The five sources **A–E** (here and on the next page) are examples of the different sorts of evidence we can use to find out what life was like in a medieval village.

Source B An artist has drawn this to show what the village of Middle Ditchford might have looked like when people lived there. What sorts of things would the artist have had to guess? What sorts of things can we still see today in other places that the artist could have drawn?

Source C The villagers could not read or write. The village priest, or a clerk, had to write down the duties and payments that the villagers owed the lord of the manor. This is an extract from the manor records of the village of Halesowen.

> The **villeins** work three days a week up to the feast of Saint Peter in August and every day up to **Michaelmas**.
>
> Agemund the miller gives 26 shillings for his mill. All the villeins provide 32 hens at Christmas.

Key words

Villeins Villagers who had to work for the lord of the manor. They were not allowed to leave the village.

Michaelmas The religious feast day of Saint Michael (29 September).

Source D Church books were often illustrated with scenes of country life. This picture shows villagers harvesting corn.

Source E Some medieval buildings still survive, and have changed very little. This is a tithe barn. Everyone in the village had to give ten per cent of their crops to the Church every year. This was called a tithe. Tithes were stored in large barns like this.

Investigations

Which of these sources can we use to find out about the following?

a) Buildings in a medieval village.
b) The work that was done in the village.
c) The important people in the village.

Village life

Evidence like that in Sources **A–E** helps to give us a good idea of what life was like in a medieval village. Let's take a walk through a typical village as it might have looked. What would we have seen?

Source F What a typical medieval village might have looked like

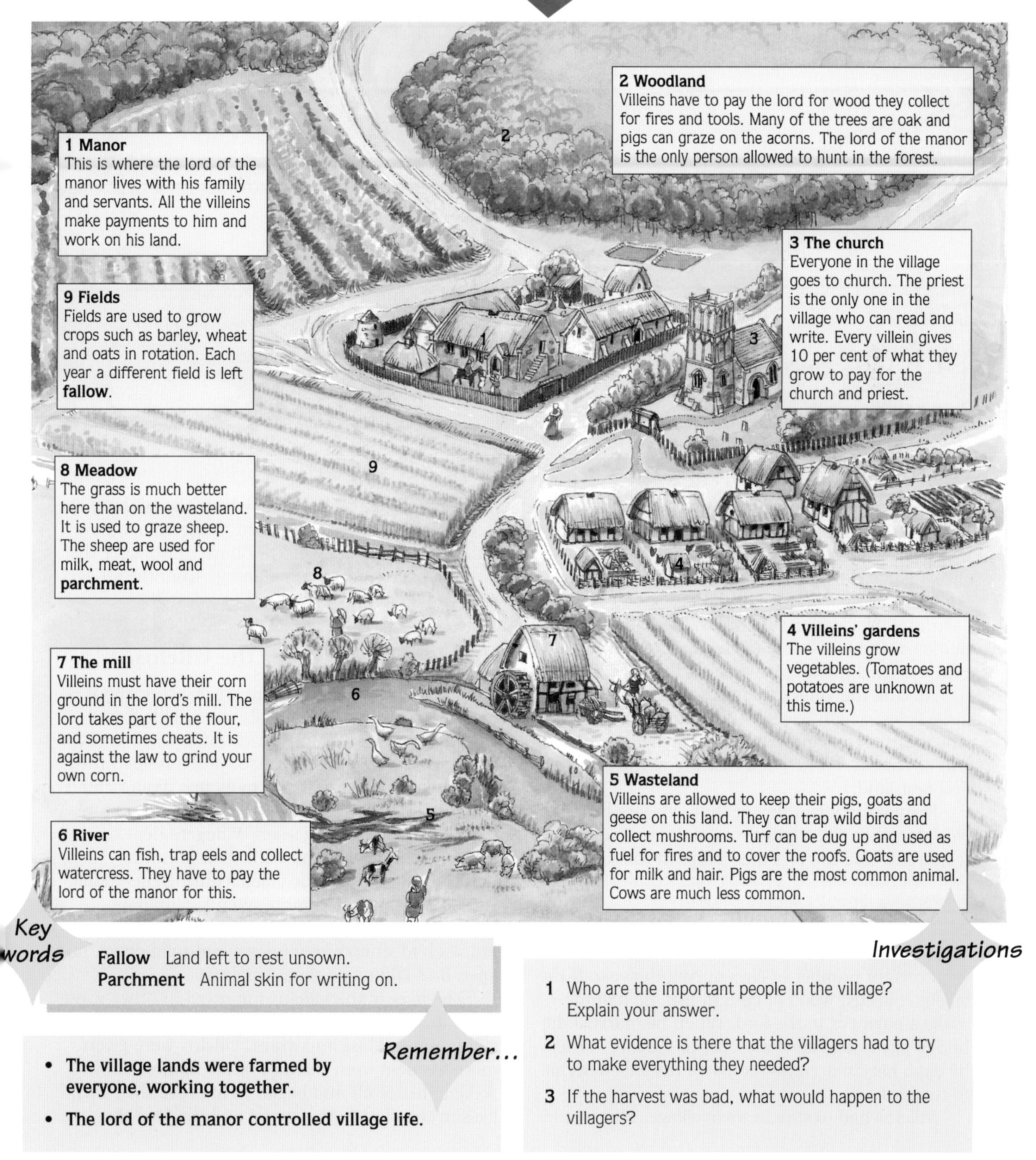

Key words

Fallow Land left to rest unsown.
Parchment Animal skin for writing on.

Remember...

- **The village lands were farmed by everyone, working together.**
- **The lord of the manor controlled village life.**

Investigations

1. Who are the important people in the village? Explain your answer.
2. What evidence is there that the villagers had to try to make everything they needed?
3. If the harvest was bad, what would happen to the villagers?

The life of a villein

- ***What was the life of a villein like?***
- ***How had the life of a villein changed by the year 1500?***

Source A Villeins working in the fields – a picture in a medieval book

Farming the land

Most of the villeins or villagers were farmers. They grew wheat (to make bread), barley (for beer), oats, rye (for animal food), vegetables and fruit. They kept sheep, goats, chickens, pigs and, sometimes, cows. Some of the villagers had other jobs such as carpenter, blacksmith and miller. Travelling to the market was difficult and often dangerous, so villagers tried to make everything they needed.

Around the village there were three or four large fields, which were divided into strips. A villein would have strips in each of the three fields. This was so that everyone got a mixture of the poorest and best land.

Farming in strips meant that villagers had to all work together at certain times of the year. Everyone would sow and harvest their crops at the same time.

The lord of the manor

The villein had to obey his lord and work for him for a certain number of days during the year. If the villein collected wood or caught fish, he had to make a payment to the lord. When he married, he had to pay a tax called merchet to the lord. When he died, his children had to pay a tax called heriot to the lord.

Villeins had to stay in their village. They could not leave to go and live somewhere else without the lord's permission. The freemen in the village were much better off. They did not have to work for the lord and were free to come and go from the village as they pleased.

Did things change for the villeins?

Villeins lived in one-room huts measuring about 6 metres by 4 metres. The walls were made from woven branches and filled with mud, straw and cow dung. There was an earth floor and a hole in the roof for smoke from the fire to escape. Water came from a nearby stream and the toilet was no more than a pit dug in the garden. Villagers slept on straw on the floor along with their animals.

Things improved for villeins during the Middle Ages. Stone was used more often for building houses, either as a foundation or for walls. More houses had shuttered windows and solid doors, but open fires still made them smokey.

The lives of the villeins improved in other ways. Their diet became healthier, although there were still famines. Most important, villeins were given more freedom from the lord of the manor. They became better off and began to improve their own lives in the clothes they wore and the food they ate.

Source B An artist's impression of what a villein's house was like in about 1500

Source C The diet of a typical villager in 1260 and 1420

Source D Sir John Fortescue, an English judge, writing in about 1460

The English are rich in gold and silver and all the things needed in life. They eat every kind of fish and meat. They are clothed with good woollens. They have plenty of bedding and are rich in all household goods.

Source E A sermon written by a priest in the fifteenth century

The common people have become very proud. A poor knave, working with a plough and a cart, used to do well with a white shirt and a red gown. Now he must have a new doublet [jacket], worth at least 5 shillings [25p], and also a costly gown with fancy trimmings and a hood. In short, those who used to work for 10 or 12 shillings [50–60p] a year now demand 20 or 30 shillings [£1.00–£1.50] and do no more work.

Remember...

- **Most people in England lived in villages in the Middle Ages.**
- **Village life was controlled by the local lord.**
- **By 1500 the lives of villeins had improved, and the lord had less control over them.**

Investigations

1 How might a villager in 1490 explain to a villager in 1080 how life has got better?

2 Examine each of the Sources **A–E** and answer the following questions.
a) What does each source tell us about life in the Middle Ages?
b) What **types** of sources are they?
c) What are the strengths and weaknesses of each of these sources in telling us about life in the Middle Ages?

Craft guilds

Many of the goods sold at markets and fairs were made by craftsmen. Making goods by hand was known as craft work. Crafts people set up stalls outside their own homes or opened up their front room as their shop. They often hung a sign outside so that people could see what they were selling.

In time these people organised themselves into guilds. A guild was rather like a modern trade union, but there was an important difference. Both the owners, who were called masters, and the workers, called journeymen, had to be members of the guild.

To become a member of a craft guild it was necessary to serve a master as an apprentice. An apprentice had to learn his trade from his master for seven years, producing 'master pieces' to prove his ability (Source **D**). He could then become a journeyman, until he eventually became a master.

Most sons usually followed the same trade as their father. They were the only people allowed to become apprentices in their trade. As the population grew, the guilds were forced to open up their membership to others.

Every guild had a charter, or set of official rules, to control its affairs. The charter would lay down rules for the following:

- The quality of the goods to be made.
- The hours per day to be worked and when work was to be done.
- Help for the old and sick members of the guild.
- Who could become a member of the guild.
- Punishment for members who had broken the rules of the guild.

A list of some of the craft guilds that might have been found in a medieval town

- Weavers
- Goldsmiths
- Saddlers
- Pewterers
- Brewers
- Tailors
- Butchers
- Shoemakers
- Dyers
- Tilers
- Arrow-makers
- Vintners (wine merchants)

Source D Apprentices show their skills to a master. What trades do you think these apprentices are learning?

Source E The Shambles in York. This street was built in medieval times. This is where the butchers had their shops. The same trades often had shops in the same street. This is a modern photograph, but it gives some idea of what streets in the Middle Ages looked like.

Source F Rules of the Cutlers' Guild in London in 1344 (cutlers made knives)

- No cutler shall sell any goods on a Sunday.
- No master shall take an apprentice for a period of less than seven years.
- All work shall be done by day and not at night, or pay a fine of 16 shillings [80p].
- No master in the trade shall take the apprentice of another until his seven years apprenticeship has been done; or pay a fine of 16 shillings.
- No cutler shall keep a shop, or take an apprentice, unless he is a freeman of the City of London.

Source G A medieval street scene. What is being sold by these traders?

Investigations

1 Choose one of the craft guilds. Use the information on these pages to design a Guild Prospectus. Design the badge for the guild and give a list of its rules.

2 Why do you think the apprentices' test piece of work was called a 'master piece'?

3 Source **E** shows a photograph of the Shambles in York. The Shambles was a street of butchers. Why would it be useful for tradespeople to group together like this? How would it benefit:

a) the tradesmen?

b) their customers?

Trade

Towns grew because of the need for merchants to trade with one another. Towns grew all over Europe as trade increased (Source **A**).

We have already seen that merchants would travel from other countries to sell their goods at fairs. This involved a long and difficult journey with the constant fear of robbery and accidents. For this reason, goods from other countries were expensive. England's most important product was wool. Before 1400, England sold raw wool abroad to be woven into cloth. This changed after 1400. England now began to send the wool abroad already woven into cloth.

Source **A** shows the type of goods England traded with other countries in Europe. People did not know that America or Australia existed at this time. However, some goods were brought from hundreds and even thousands of miles away.

Spices, which came from India, were very important. Some animals had to be killed in the autumn as there was not enough food to keep them alive during the winter. Spices were needed to stop the meat from rotting and to make the dried meat more tasty.

Rich people could afford to drink Italian and French wines, and wear clothes made from Italian silks.

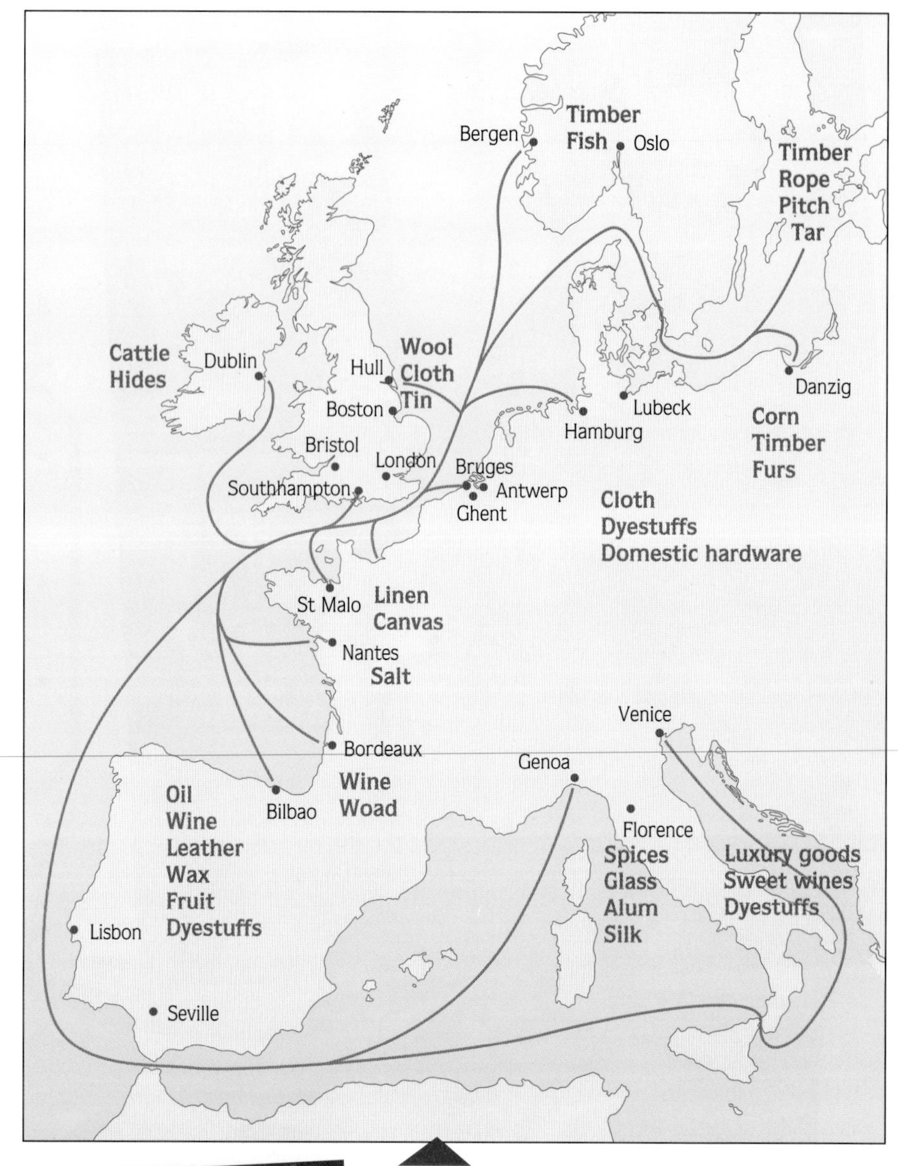

Source A Trade in medieval Europe

Source B Medieval merchants and their ships in the German city of Hamburg. What kinds of goods might these ships be carrying?

Remember...

- **Towns grew up as centres of trade.**
- **Towns offered greater freedom for those who lived in them.**

Investigations

1 Look at Source **A**.
a) What are the main items of trade?
b) What would these have been used for?

The church

Source A A parish priest pictured in a stained-glass window in All Saints' Church, York

How important was the church in medieval society?

The parish priest

Nearly every town and village had a church which the local people had helped to build. Every Sunday they went there to attend **mass**.

The **parish** priest was probably the only person in the village who could read and write. During church services he would read from the Bible which was written in Latin, the official language of the Catholic Church. Few people would be able to understand what the words meant.

To help people understand, wall paintings and stained-glass windows in the church would show stories from the Bible. The congregation would sit or kneel on the floor, or stand, for few churches had seats.

The parish priest would help the sick, the poor and those in trouble. In return, he expected the people in the parish to respect him, obey his instructions and pay their tithe (see page 60).

Source B Wall-painting of heaven and hell. It shows good people in heaven, and evil-doers in hell.

Source C This is part of a popular medieval story written in France in about 1200. A man called Aucassin has just been told that he might go to hell if he keeps on seeing his girlfriend, Nicolette. This is his answer.

> Why should I want to go to heaven? I would not wish to go there unless I can have Nicolette, because I love her so much. I want nothing to do with those people who want to go to heaven, doddering old priests and fools who grovel in church all day and night. I'd rather be in hell with those handsome knights killed in battle and other noble men, with those lovely ladies who have lots of lovers.

Key words

Mass The most important church service, in which worshippers share bread and wine in memory of the death of Jesus.
Parish The local area for which a church and its priest are responsible.

Investigations

1. Draw a spider diagram about 'The Parish Priest'. Around the title write down all the jobs the priest would be expected to do. Why would this make him an important person in the parish?
2. What would people have learnt about the Church from the images in Sources **A** and **B**?
3. Read Source **C**.
   a) This story is very popular. What can this tell us about people's attitude to the Church in medieval times?
   b) Why might many people have found it hard to obey the teachings of the Church?

Monks and nuns

Monks and nuns were men and women who took a vow – a promise to God – to live apart from other people, and to dedicate their lives to prayer and worshipping God (Source **E**). Monks lived in monasteries, and nuns lived in convents. Most monasteries and convents were small, with only a few monks or nuns living there. Some were much larger, like Fountains and Rievaulx in Yorkshire, and Hexham in Northumberland. These were called abbeys.

Monasteries, convents and abbeys were often built in remote places, far from other people. Monks and nuns lived by strict rules, and their living conditions were very hard. There was only heating in one room, and no personal possessions were allowed. Neither monks nor nuns were allowed to marry.

By 1300 there were 12 500 monks and 7 000 nuns in England (roughly one in every 150 people).

Source D Some monks did not live up to the rules of their order. They were criticised for this. This shows what some monks could not resist. It comes from a thirteenth-century manuscript.

Why were monks and nuns often unpopular?

In time, however, many abbeys became quite rich. Monks and nuns did not work for money. Larger monasteries and abbeys often owned valuable farm land, for which they charged rent. Many kept sheep, and sold the wool. Rich people often gave gifts to the monasteries and convents in the hope that they would be favoured by God.

Sometimes monks and nuns did not keep to the strict rules of their **order**. Monks often left their monastery to eat and drink in the local tavern, or meet women. Some nuns were even known to have children!

However, most followed the rules of their order, and led a life of devotion and serving others. They helped the poor and the sick, and gave shelter to travellers.

Timetable

2.00 a.m.	Nocturns
Daybreak	Matins
6.00 a.m.	Prime
8.30 a.m.	Tierce
11.30 a.m.	Sext
12.00 noon	Midday meal
14.30 p.m.	Nones
17.30 p.m.	Evening meal
18.00 p.m.	Vespers
20.00 p.m.	Compline
20.15 p.m.	Bedtime

Source E A monk's day. Monks (and nuns) were required to take part in church services throughout the day. Between Matins and Compline they were expected to work.

Key words

Order A group of monks or nuns that lives by a particular rule.

Source F Monks singing in church. How many times a day would monks have to do this (look at Source **E**)?

Source G The growth in the number of monasteries

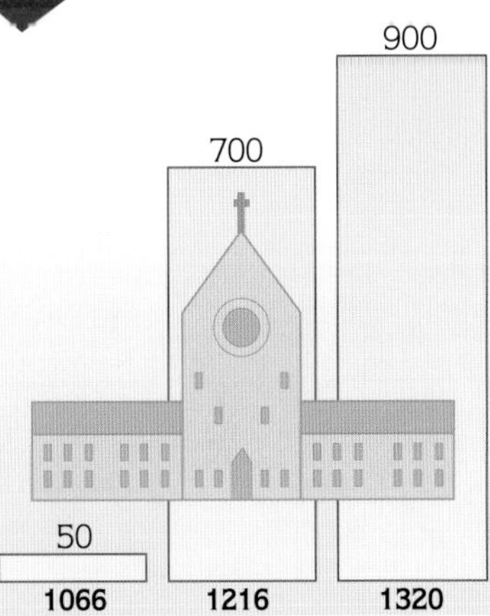

Source H The Rule of Saint Benedict. Saint Benedict lived in the twelfth century and began one of the most famous orders of monks, called the Benedictines.

Rules of Saint Benedict

- To spend your whole life praying and working for God.
- To give away everything you own.
- To obey the abbot (head of the monastery) in all things.
- To wear a monk's habit (robe) and sandals and to have the top of the head shaved (this was known as a 'tonsure').
- To remain in the monastery until you die.
- Never to marry.

Source I From the *Canterbury Tales* by Geoffrey Chaucer. These stories were written in the fourteenth century. This extract describes a nun.

She was called Madam Eglantine and she sang well in church. She had small dogs as pets and she fed them roast meat, milk and expensive bread. She cried if one of the dogs got hurt. She always made sure she looked her best and wore jewellery of coral and gold.

Investigations

1. Why do you think the lives of monks and nuns were made so hard? (Use Sources **E** and **H** to help with your answer.)
2. What evidence is there that people thought monks and nuns were important (Source **G**)?
3. What criticisms were made of monks and nuns (Sources **D** and **I**)?
4. Why do you think that not all monks and nuns were well behaved?
5. Draw a pair of scales. On one side write what you think are the good points, on the other the bad points, about monks and nuns. Does your scale tip in favour or against them? Is there any other evidence on these pages to make a difference to your judgement?

The friars

While monks and nuns lived apart from other people, friars did the opposite. Their purpose was to live in large towns and cities, among people. Friars helped the sick and the poor, and preached to ordinary people about God. They taught, by their example, how God cared for everyone.

The most famous orders of friars were the Franciscans – founded by St Francis – and the Dominicans, founded by St Dominic.

Friars lived together in houses called friaries, which they often built themselves. Friaries were often built on land given to the friars by the wealthy noblemen and merchants of the town.

Friars took a vow to live in poverty. They were often given gifts of food and clothing because people appreciated the work they did.

Like monks and nuns, some friars got a reputation for having girlfriends and enjoying drinking and eating. You will be familiar with the character of Friar Tuck, in the stories of Robin Hood.

Source J St Francis, the founder of the most famous order of friars. All Franciscan friars wore the same kind of robe as that worn by St Francis.

Source K Friar Tuck, as portrayed in the film *The Adventures of Robin Hood*

Source L What friars were supposed to do

Investigations

You are the abbot in charge of Friar Tuck's friary. You have heard how he spends his time in the local tavern, in the company of local women. What would you tell him to remind him of his vows as a friar?

5 Life and death in medieval society

Disease and illness

- ***What did people think caused diseases and illness?***
- ***What treatment was given to sick people?***

The chances of a long life

Today many of us expect to live a long life. If we are ill, we get help from doctors. To understand about illness in medieval times you must try to forget everything you now take for granted. If you escaped illness and accident you might live to an old age. If you were rich you might expect to live twice as long than if you were poor.

Half the babies born died before they were one year old. A person aged 40 was considered very old.

Source A Medieval medical treatment

Midwives had no proper training

Only the rich could afford doctors. Doctors knew nothing about germs, and worked in unclean conditions.

Doctors had no knowledge of **inoculation** or **vaccination**. Instead they relied on traditional **herbal** remedies and medicines.

Surgeons had no **anaesthetics** or **antiseptics**. Patients were made drowsy with wine for an operation or **amputation**.

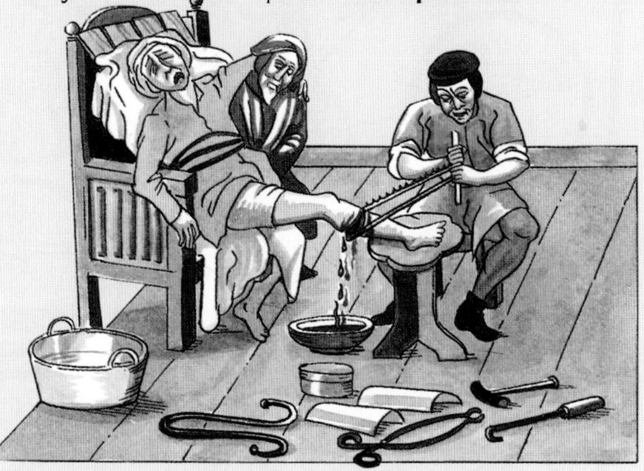

Key words

Midwife A person, usually a woman, who helps deliver babies.
Inoculation/Vaccination Injections to help fight disease.
Herbal Made from plants and herbs.
Anaesthetic A drug to put a patient to sleep before an operation.
Antiseptic Chemicals used to kill germs.
Amputation An operation to remove an arm or a leg.

What did medieval doctors believe caused disease and illness?

Ideas about disease had not changed for one thousand years, since the time of the Ancient Greeks. The Ancient Greeks believed the body was made up of four 'humours' – earth, air, fire and water. If you had too much or too little of one of the humours, then you became ill. To get well you needed to restore the right balance between the humours.

How did doctors try to find out what was wrong with people?

The colour of a patient's urine was thought to help tell doctors what was wrong with them (Source **C**). However, this was more usually affected by the food and drink the patient had recently had.

The stars were thought to affect different parts of the body. The doctor would want to know the patient's birth sign, to help him decide why they were ill (Source **D**).

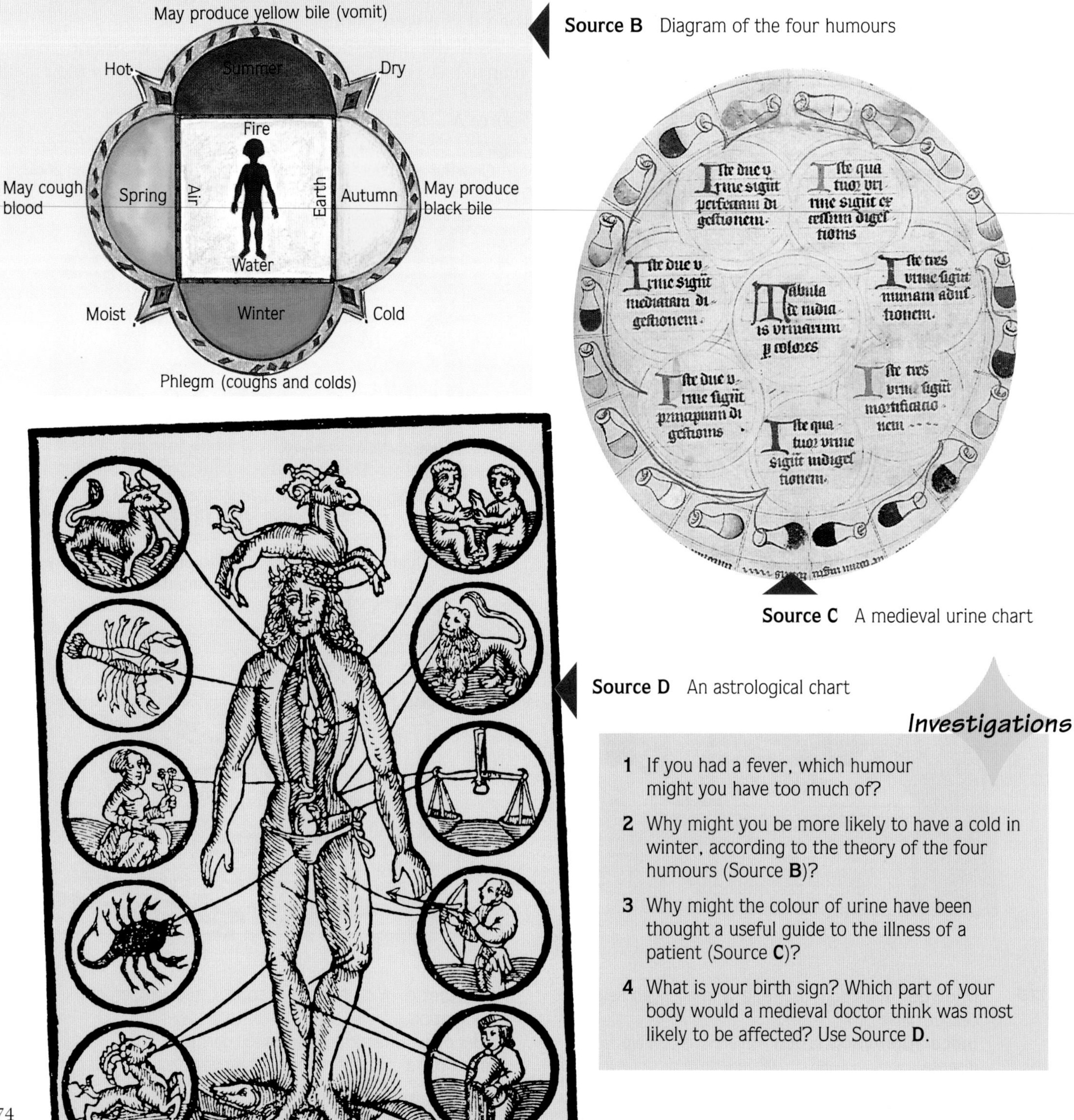

Source B Diagram of the four humours

Source C A medieval urine chart

Source D An astrological chart

Investigations

1. If you had a fever, which humour might you have too much of?
2. Why might you be more likely to have a cold in winter, according to the theory of the four humours (Source **B**)?
3. Why might the colour of urine have been thought a useful guide to the illness of a patient (Source **C**)?
4. What is your birth sign? Which part of your body would a medieval doctor think was most likely to be affected? Use Source **D**.

Medical treatment

Some doctors were highly skilled and could perform simple operations where the cause was fairly obvious – for example, if a damaged limb had to be amputated (Source **E**).

Letting a patient bleed was thought to help make them well. Patients were bled either by opening a vein with a sharp knife or attaching a blood-sucking leech to the patient's body (Source **F**).

Poor people couldn't afford doctors, so they relied on herbs, which they often gathered themselves or bought from an **apothecary** (Source **I**). Herbs were made up into potions to drink or were laid on sores and wounds. Many herbal medicines are still in use today. The juice from poppies contains morphine which helps to deaden pain, and garlic helps the blood to flow faster.

Source E A doctor amputating a man's leg

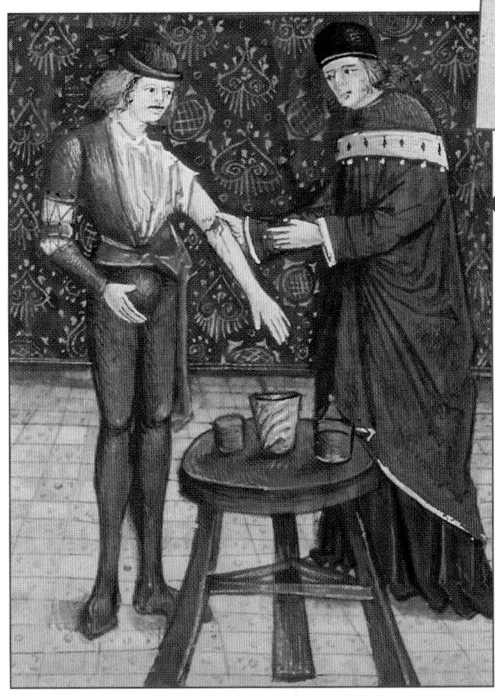

Source F A patient being bled by a doctor

Religion and illness

The Church and the Bible taught people that illness was God's punishment for being wicked.

Sick people tried to make amends by praying, giving gifts to the Church, or helping others. Many went on a **pilgrimage**. Sick people would travel many miles to pray at holy places, usually connected with a saint. The most famous of these was Thomas Becket's tomb at Canterbury. Sick people still visit famous shrines today, such as at Lourdes in France.

Source G Patients being looked after by nuns

Source H A doctor performing a nose operation

Key words

Apothecary Someone who made and sold medicines and potions.

Pilgrimage A journey to a holy place, such as the tomb of a saint.

Source I An apothecary collecting herbs for remedies

Source J Medieval herbal cures

- Take a fat cat and skin it. Mix together hedgehog grease, bear fat, herbs, honeysuckle and wax. Stuff the cat with the mixture then roast it. Take the grease and rub it in.
- Collect some crickets and cut off the heads and wings. Put them in a pot of oil along with dung beetles. Heat the mixture, then crush it and rub it on any painful parts.
- Shave the head and smear with the grease of a fox. If this fails, wash the scalp with the juice of beetles.
- Wear the skin of a donkey.
- Take the gall bladder of a hare and the grease of a fox. Warm the mixture and place in the ear.
- Boil a red haired dog in oil, add worms and pigs' marrow. Make a mixture and put it on the swollen foot.
- Put your finger on the tooth and repeat the Lord's Prayer.
- Take a cockerel for a sick boy or a hen for a sick girl. Throw 4d into the well and say the Lord's Prayer. The disease will pass out of the child into the bird.

I recently asked a friend why he was no longer a doctor. He replied, 'If people knew how little we actually help a patient, the company of doctors would be much smaller. Let them promise life, even though they often kill. But I don't want to cheat and kill; I don't want to get richer by doing other people harm'.

Source K A doctor's opinion. By Alfredo Matti in a letter written in 1365.

Remember...

- **Doctors did not know that germs caused illness.**
- **It was believed that illness was caused by too much or too little of one of the four humours.**
- **People took herbal medicines when they were ill.**
- **Illness was believed to be a punishment from God.**

Investigations

1 Why might some types of treatment work because they are based on common sense?

2 Look at Source **G**.
a) How might the conditions in the nunnery help patients to recover?
b) How can you tell from this picture that the nuns did not understand what caused diseases to spread?

3 How did doctors believe they were helping a patient by bleeding him (Source **F**)?
Clue: Think of the four humours in Source **B**.

4 Can you match the cures in Source **J** to the following illnesses? (Some can be used twice.)
• tonsilitis • swollen flesh • baldness • rheumatism
• earache • gout (swollen foot) • toothache

5 Why did religion play such an important part in curing illness? (Think of the importance of Christian belief and how much doctor's knew about disease.)

6 If these cures did not work, why might people still continue to use them?

7 Read Source **K**. Why is this a useful piece of evidence about doctors' knowledge of illness?

The Black Death

What was the Black Death?

The arrival of the Black Death

In 1348 a tidal wave of fear swept through Europe. It was caused by the arrival of a mysterious and terrible disease which people at the time called the 'Black Death'. At least one third of the population of Europe died, and perhaps as much as a half.

The disease did not go away. For the next three hundred and fifty years the disease – also known as the **plague** – would break out, from time to time, into dreadful **epidemics**. These epidemics would carry off the rich as well as the poor.

How did it kill people?

The Black Death was caused by two types of plague. Both still exist today.

- **Bubonic Plague** This was the most common plague. It is a germ carried in the bloodstream of rats. Fleas bite the rats and become infected with the disease. They then hop onto humans, bite them, and pass on the disease. Large swellings, called buboes, appear in the victim's groin and armpits. About 70 per cent of those who catch the disease die. Victims usually die within four to seven days of becoming ill.
- **Pneumonic Plague** This is a more deadly plague, and is caught by breathing in the germs. It affects the lungs, and when patients cough or sneeze the infected blood is carried to those nearby. Victims suffer a fever, and die after about two days.

Where did it come from?

The Black Death came to England through trade. It travelled from China and India through the Middle East to Europe, following the **trade routes**. Ships carrying infected people and infected rats landed at ports across Europe.

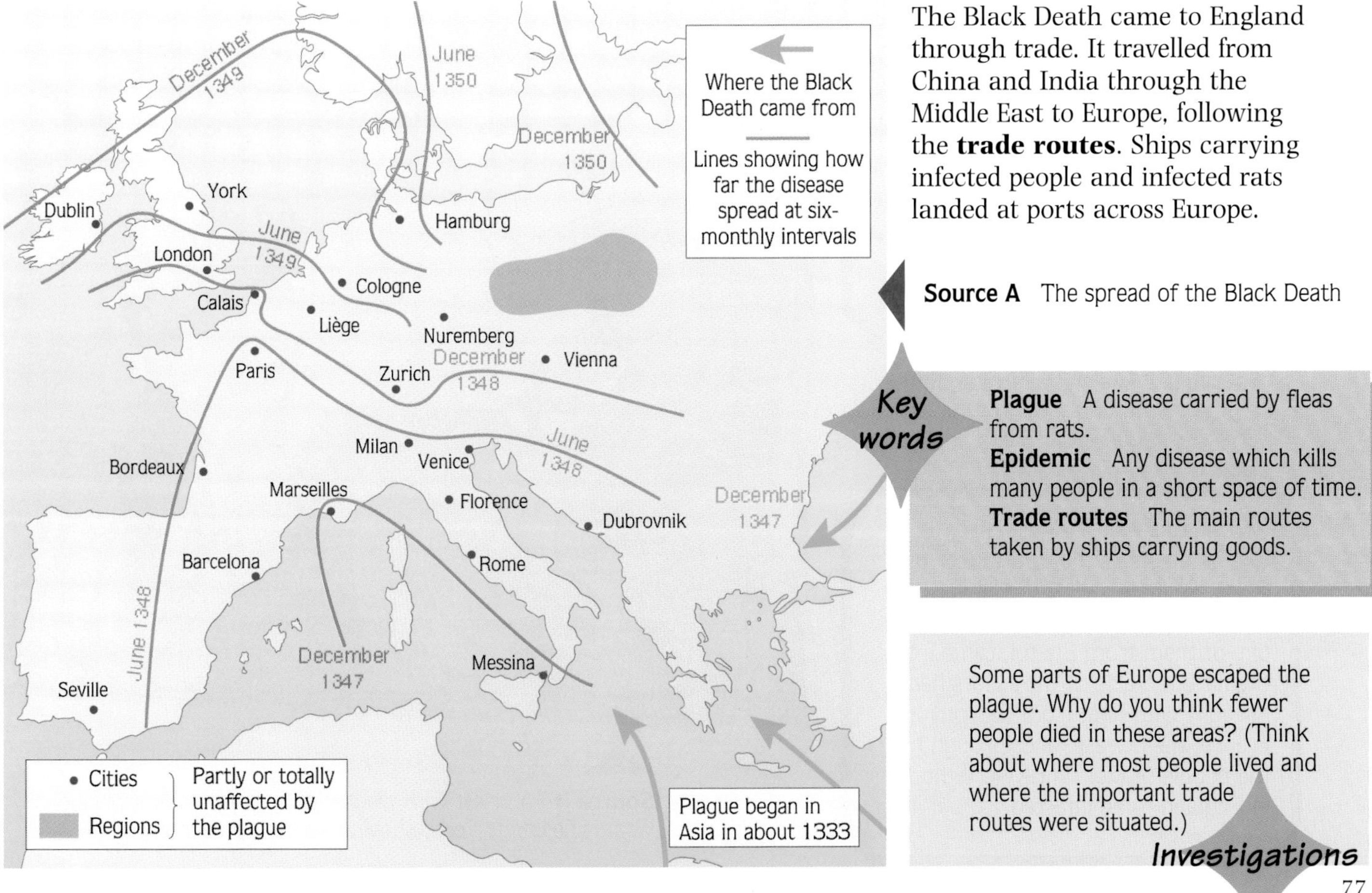

Source A The spread of the Black Death

Key words

Plague A disease carried by fleas from rats.
Epidemic Any disease which kills many people in a short space of time.
Trade routes The main routes taken by ships carrying goods.

Some parts of Europe escaped the plague. Why do you think fewer people died in these areas? (Think about where most people lived and where the important trade routes were situated.)

Investigations

How did the disease spread?

Source B A description of the plague in India in 1345, written by the chronicler of the Italian town of Este

In the East in a place near India there were horrors and storms for three days. On the first day, out of the sky fell frogs, snakes, lizards, scorpions and other poisonous animals. On the second day there was thunder and lightening. Sheets of fire and huge hailstones fell on the earth. On the third day fire and stinking smoke came down from heaven. This killed all the remaining men and animals and destroyed all the towns.

Source C The plague strikes a town by the Black Sea in Russia, in December 1347

The Italian merchants and others crowded together inside the walls of the town. They could hardly breathe. They were helped when a ship arrived, bringing them food. Then plague broke out among the **Tartars** who were laying **siege** to the town. The Tartars used giant catapults to fling the dead bodies into the town.

Source D The plague reaches Genoa in Italy in 1348. By Boccaccio, a famous writer who was in Genoa while the plague was there.

In January of the year 1348 three galleys [ships] put in at Genoa. They had come from the East and were horribly infected with the plague. No one would go near the ships even though they had a valuable cargo of spices and other goods.

Source E The plague reaches France in August 1348. By Jean de Venette, a French friar.

In the month of August 1348, after the evening sun began to set, a very bright star appeared above Paris, towards the west. The star seemed much nearer the earth than stars usually are. As the sun set and night came on, it seemed to me and the other friars who were watching that the star stayed in one place. At last darkness fell. Then to the amazement of all of us, the star split up into many different rays. It shed these rays towards the east, over Paris. The star then completely disappeared.

Source F The arrival of the plague in England in 1348. From the *Chronicle* of Henry Knighton, 1349.

Then the dreadful disease reached England. It started at Southampton and spread along the coast. It reached Bristol where almost everyone in the town died.

Source G The plague arrives on the south coast of England. From the *Grey Friars Chronicle*, 1348.

In this year, at Melcombe [Weymouth] in the county of Dorset, a little before the feast of St John the Baptist [24 June], two ships, one of them from Bristol, came into the harbour. One of the sailors had brought with him, from Gascony in France, the disease, and through him the people of Melcombe were the first in England to be infected.

Source H A priest with plague victims. Why might plague victims be comforted by having a priest with them?

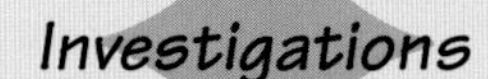

1 Match each of these illustrations with
a) one of the sources **B–G**;
b) one of the places labelled on the map (make a list of the completed names).

2 How do the sources help us to understand the way in which the plague spread?

3 Sources **B** and **E** describe fantastic events which surrounded the appearance of the plague. Why do you think this is? (Think about how much people at the time knew about the plague and its terrible effects.)

4 Some of these sources were written by church writers. What does this tell you about what they thought had caused the plague?

5 In what ways do Sources **F** and **G** disagree? What possible reasons might there be for this? (Think about the reasons why it was difficult for news to spread.)

Key words

Tartars Wild tribesmen who came from Asia and attacked Russia.
Siege Surrounding a town to try and starve the people inside and force them to surrender.

Class activities

6 Chain of Death

There are 6 sources on these two pages which together describe the route the plague took.

- Choose six pairs from the class. Each pair is to study one of the sources carefully.
- The teacher (or another pupil) represents the Black Death. 'Black Death' passes a black spot or buboe to each of the pairs of pupils in turn. They then tell the class what happened when the disease arrived at the place in their source.

7 Chroniclers of Death

The same arrangement as in Activity 6. For this activity the rest of the class are divided into pairs.

- They visit each of the six pairs in turn and ask them their name, when they wrote their source, and what information they can give.
- The information is recorded and then arranged in the right order.

Are there any other questions you would like to ask the witnesses?

What did people think caused the Black Death?

At this time doctors did not know that germs caused disease. They looked for all sorts of reasons to explain why something so terrible should have happened.

It is important to remember that most people in Europe at this time were Christians. They believed that God knew everything that happened, and that many things happened because God wanted them to happen.

The following sources show the different ways in which people tried to explain the cause of the Black Death.

Source I Contact with plague victims, by Jean de Venette

> Throughout the years 1348 and 1349 huge numbers of people died, both men and women, and the young more than the old. People who were completely healthy became ill for only two or three days and then died. Someone who was well one day may be dead the next and being carried to his grave.
>
> The disease was spread because of **contagion**. If a healthy man visited the plague victim, he usually died himself.

Source J Punishment from God – by an unknown Italian writer

> The plague carried by these cursed Italian galleys was a punishment sent by God. He did this because these galleys had helped the Unbelievers [**Muslims**] capture a Christian town. The Italian merchants had broken down the walls and killed their fellow Christians.

> In many German cities Jews were believed to have caused the deaths [from the plague] by poisoning the wells. Many of these unbelievers [Jews], including women and children, were burnt, after pleading with them to accept the true faith of Christ. Many Jews were moneylenders, and people saw a way of wiping out their **debts** in the flames.

Source K **Jews** – from the *Neuberg Chronicle*

Source L A medieval wall-painting in a French church

Investigations

1. Write down this sentence and fill in the gaps.

   I think the most sensible explanation for the cause of the Black Death is Source ____ because ____.

2. Why do you think some medieval Christians blamed Jews and Muslims for causing the Black Death? (Sources **J** and **K**).
3. What other reasons did some people have for blaming the Jews?
4. Look closely at the painting in Source **L**.
   a) What different sorts of people can you see in the picture?
   b) What does the hooded figure in the middle represent?
   c) What is this painting saying about the Black Death?

Key words

Contagion Disease spread by contact between people.
Muslims People who believe in God, whom they call Allah. They are the followers of a prophet called Muhammad (see page 54) whom they believe was a messenger from God.
Jews People who believe in God, but do not believe that Jesus Christ was the son of God.
Debts Money that is owed.

How did people try to cure the plague?

Without a knowledge of germs, medieval doctors relied upon plants and herbal cures to fight the disease. However, because they were unable to stop the spread of the plague, many people begged God to help them.

These sources show some of the ways that people tried to fight the plague.

Source N Drawing out the plague. By Guy de Chauliac.

Toads should be thoroughly dried in the sun. They should be placed on the plague boil. The toad will swell and draw out the poison of the plague to its own body. When it is full it should be thrown away and a new one applied.

Source M Some practical advice to prevent plague. By the Bishop of Arhus, in Denmark

Let your house be clean and make a fire of flaming wood.

Source O Cure for buboes. By Guy de Chauliac, a French friar.

For cures, bleeding and making the patient vomit should be attempted. The swellings should be softened with figs and cooked onions, mixed with yeast and butter. The swellings should be cut open and treated like ulcers.

Source P Asking for God's help. By Jean de Venette.

People gathered together in large groups and marched in procession, with their backs bare. When they got to the crossroads, or the market square of towns they formed circles and beat their backs with weighted whips until they drew blood. They sang loudly, and many of these hymns were completely new. They asked God to forgive them their sins, but after a little time everyone stopped doing this.

Source Q
A medieval picture of **flagellants**. Why did people choose to punish themselves in this way?

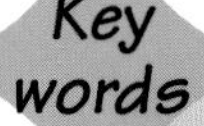

Key words

Flagellants
People who believed that if they whipped and hurt themselves God would take pity on them and forgive them for their sins.

Investigations

Imagine that you live in medieval times. You and your family are afraid of catching the plague.

a) Look at the suggested cures to be found in these sources. Decide which ones you and your family would try. (Remember you are living in medieval times, *not* modern times.)
b) Give your decision, and the reasons for your choice of cures, in a table like this.

	Will try	Will not try	Reason
Source M			
Source N			
Source O			
Source P			

How did people behave during the plague?

Faced with such a terrible disease, people behaved in very different ways. Some tried to help those who suffered from the plague. Others looked after themselves first.

Source R Religious people. By Jean de Venette.

For a long time more than five hundred corpses a day were carried in carts to the cemetery of the Holy Innocents. The saintly nuns were not afraid of death and a great number of them died giving their own lives to help the victims.

This was not as true for many priests, and many of them fled.

Source S Doctors. By Guy de Chauliac.

Doctors were useless and indeed shameful, especially as they dared not visit the sick for fear of catching the disease.

It is said that the world was changed for the worse. People were meaner and more grasping than before, even though they had more things. They were jealous and there was an increase in the number of fights and arguments.

Source T Change for the worse. By Jean de Venette.

Source U Wild living. By Matteo Villani of Florence, 1349.

The few people who remained alive led wild and wicked lives. They did no work but spent their time eating vast meals. They drank and feasted on expensive foods. They gambled and dressed in strange clothes.

Investigations

1. **Survival**. Imagine that the plague has struck your village and you are worried about the health of your family. You must make a decision. Would you:
   - stay together and remain in the village;
   - escape from the village with your family (and maybe carry the plague with you);
   - arrange for your children to be taken to a relative, where the plague has not struck, while you remain in the village.

   Explain the reasons for your decision.
2. What kinds of things do the writers of these sources accuse many people of doing? What reasons might there be for many people behaving like this?
3. Sources **R**, **S** and **T** are written by church people. Why might they want to accuse people of behaving badly?
4. Which people in society would have been expected to help others at the time of the Black Death? If they had not given this help, how might others have felt?

Source V A drinking party, shown in a French painting in 1349. Why might the plague have made people behave in this way?

Remember...

- **The Black Death killed at least one third, and maybe half, of the population of Europe.**
- **It was carried by fleas from rats.**
- **It was spread by travellers on the main trade routes.**

The effects of the Black Death

How did the Black Death affect medieval society?

A disaster as great as the Black Death was bound to change medieval society. However, historians do not agree about just what these changes were.

To begin with, it is difficult to agree about how many people died of the plague. No records were kept, and therefore we do not know exactly how many people lived in Europe at the time, or how many died.

Did living and working conditions get better for the peasants because of the Black Death? With fewer people left to work on the land, did their wages rise for those who were left? Were they able to pay money to the lord instead of doing **week work** on his land? If so, this would allow them the freedom to work harder on their own land and make more money.

Historians can't agree about the answers to these questions, or about what the effects of the Black Death were.

Look at Sources **A–C**. Do they give us any clues?

How many people died?

Source A English population, 1100–1525

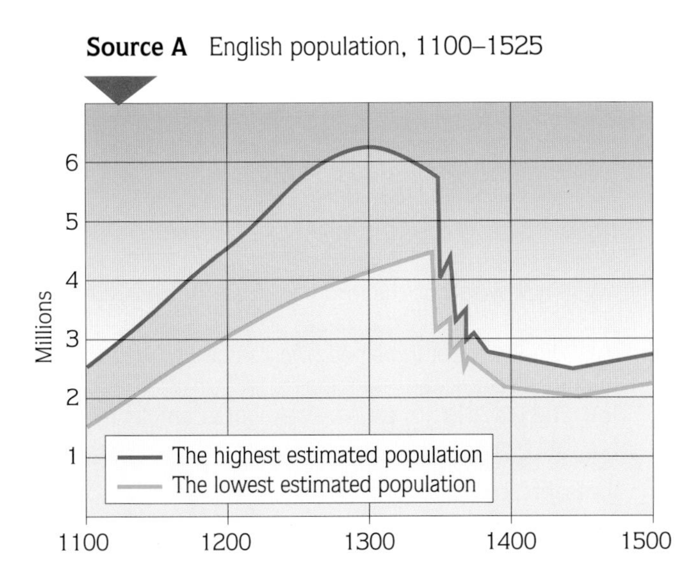

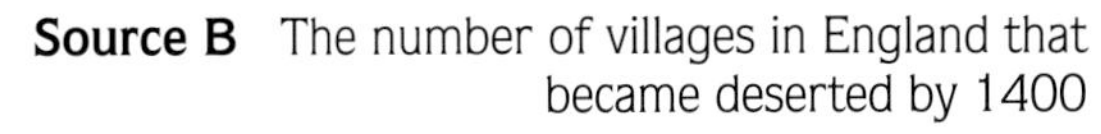

Source B The number of villages in England that became deserted by 1400

Source C A smaller population. From the court roll for the Manor of Sladen, Buckinghamshire, 1349.

A jury in August 1349 declared that the mill was of no value, for not only was the miller dead, but there were no tenants who wanted to grind any corn. The total **rents** of freemen and serfs in the previous year amounted to £12. This year nothing has been collected.

Key words

Week work Every peasant had to work on the lord's land, usually for about three days every week.
Rents Peasants could make a money payment to the lord instead of doing week work.

How did working life change?

Source D The king attempts to keep wages down. From the Statute of Labourers 1349. This same law was passed five times between 1349 and 1381. (Remember that Members of Parliament were landowners.)

Labourers should not be paid more than they used to receive before the plague.

Year	Number of unpaid people at harvest	Money in wages
1348	121	none
1349	60	£3.50
1350	28	£3.50

(By 1376 tenants' rents had been raised from 25p to 33p but no one is forced to work on the lord's land without payment in wages.)

Source E Wages paid to harvesters

Source F Wages and week work. Evidence from Elton manor.

Source G The price of wheat (per quarter of a ton) from manors in Hampshire and Somerset

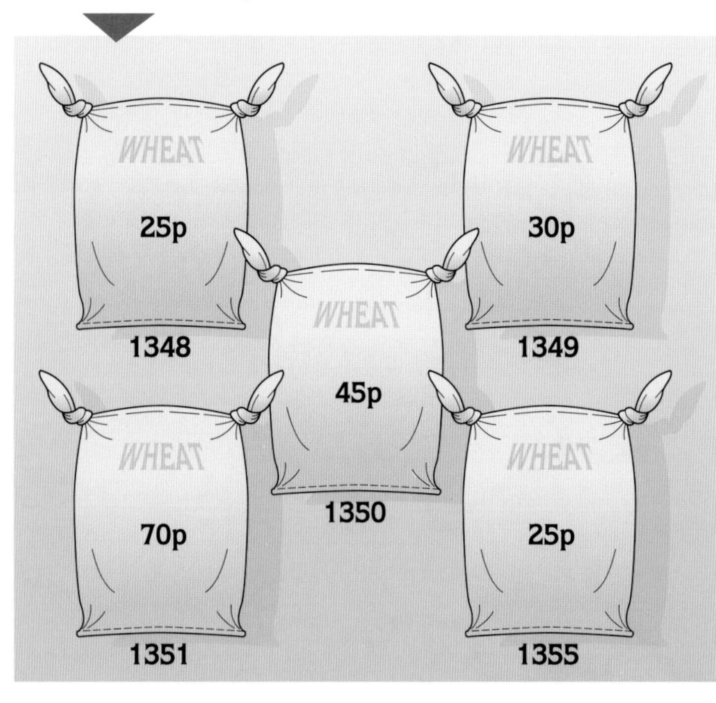

Source H Wages of farm workers

Year	Reaping	Threshing
1346	3p	2p
1349	3p	2p
1353	8p	2p

Investigations

1 Your group or class has been asked to explain how the Black Death changed medieval society.

- What do you think are the two most important questions historians need to ask when investigating the effects of the Black Death?
- What are the problems in trying to put together the evidence? (Are there accurate records of the population? Does the evidence from one place tell us about what happened everywhere?)

Bearing these questions in mind, explain why you agree or disagree with each of the following statements.

a) Week work for the lord had disappeared before the plague.

b) The Black Death helped bring an end to week work more quickly.

c) The Black Death ended week work completely.

2 Divide the class into two groups. One group are the peasants, the other are the lords. Each group is to make a list of:

a) the ways in which their life has got better as a result of the Black Death;

b) the ways in which it has made things worse for them.

Remember...

- **Historians do not agree about the effects of the Black Death.**
- **Most historians agree that the Black Death helped bring an end to the feudal system.**

6 Our medieval heritage

Medieval artists and craftsmen

Who made medieval works of art?

Medieval times have left us a wonderful **heritage** of works of art including buildings, paintings, hand-made crafts, clothes, writing, and songs. Most were made for a purpose rather than for their own sake.

Since nearly everyone was Christian, the main purpose of art, was to celebrate the Glory of God. The Church was the main **patron** of artists, and many found work building or decorating the magnificent cathedrals and abbeys that sprang up across Europe. On a smaller scale, nearly every town wanted a grand church. Other work was ordered by kings, nobles or rich merchants. Fine clothes, hand-written books or even a castle or palace in the latest style, helped the owner show off their wealth or power.

We sometimes know about the history of a work of art, or who ordered it to be made. However, we usually know little or nothing about the person who made it. Before the fifteenth century, artists were not seen as special. They were respected as good **craftsworkers** in their trade but were no more important, or better paid, than other skilled people such as bakers, blacksmiths or builders. However, we can piece together information about how artists worked from looking at paintings or illuminated manuscripts, like those in Sources **B**, **D**, **E** and **F**.

Source A Inside the great Norman cathedral at Durham. Building work began in 1093 and lasted for nearly 40 years.

Source B Stone masons and builders in about 1250

Source C King Richard II ordered a painting of the baby Jesus and the Virgin Mary. The unknown artist included the king in the picture. Can you identify the king?

Key words

Heritage Things that have survived from the past.
Patron People who support artists by paying them to do work.
Craftsworker A skilled worker, usually a guild member (see Chapter 4).

Source D The **miracle** of a **mural** painter saved from death, painted in a thirteenth-century Spanish manuscript

1. How the devil appeared to the painter and threatened him for painting him ugly.
2. How all the people gave thanks to St Mary for the miracle she had done.
3. How a painter painted a very beautiful image of St Mary and an ugly one of the devil.
4. How people came and saw the painter suspended in the air.
5. How the painter painted an image of Mary on the vault.
6. How the devil destroyed the scaffold, but the painter remained suspended on the painting.

Key words

Miracle Something made to happen by the power of God and saints.
Mural Painting on a wall or ceiling.

Source E Glassmakers at work in the fifteenth century

Source F A woman artist painting Mary and Jesus. Women were not usually allowed to join craft guilds, except perhaps as widows taking their husband's place.

Source G Advice to artists, from a manual written in about 1500

> Most people decorate walls with golden tin, because it costs less. But I say always decorate with fine gold and with good colours, especially in the figure of Our Lady [Mary]. You may reply that a poor person cannot afford this. I answer that if you do your work well you will get a good reputation and sell to a wealthy person.

Remember...

- **Medieval craftspeople were highly skilled.**
- **Much of their work was done for the Church or other wealthy patrons.**
- **Many medieval artists are unknown.**

Investigations

1. Look at Source **A**. This shows the nave or main area of the cathedral. How would this have impressed those who were going to worship?
2. Think about Source **C**. Why do you think King Richard wanted to be in the picture with the Virgin Mary and baby Jesus?
3. Look at Source **B**. List the tools and machinery you can see in use on this building site. What would be the same and what would be different today?
4. The captions under Source **D** are in the wrong order. Write them out so that they match the order of the scenes in the picture.
5. How can we tell that the woman in Source **F** is in charge? What is the other person doing?
6. Why does the writer in Source **G** think it is wrong for an artist to do cheap work?
7. You are a nobleman planning to pay for a new local church. What work will need to be done, and what craftsworkers will you need to hire? Use Sources **B** to **G** to help you.

Chivalry: the art of being a knight

How did chivalry affect the way knights behaved?

Were knights really chivalrous?

Have you ever been told to behave like a gentleman or a lady? This idea of good conduct has been passed down to us from medieval times. The Middle Ages is sometimes called 'The Age of Chivalry' by historians. The word 'chivalry' comes from the French word *chevalerie*, meaning 'horsemanship'. By the tenth century, however, it had come to mean a code of conduct for knights – a way of controlling their violence and making them behave properly.

Knights were the best warriors in Europe. They took years to train and their armour, weapons and horses were expensive. The feudal system gave knights land to meet their costs, in return for fighting for their king or lord.

The code of chivalry tried to make possible an orderly world in which knights protected the weak and left their fighting for tournaments, as Sources **A** to **D** show. The Church supported this by declaring the 'Peace of God' on days when no fighting was allowed, and encouraging knights to save their energies for Crusades (see Chapter 5). Minstrels and poets made chivalry glamorous by telling stories of the adventures of King Arthur, or of Roland, who was a famous French knight.

Most knights knew how they *should* behave, but reality – as you can see in Sources **F** to **H** – was often different. Wars were common and during peaceful times knights picked quarrels with their neighbours. Their power was based on their skill with weapons, and they looked for opportunities to use them.

Source A By John of Salisbury, in the fourteenth century

> What is knighthood for? To protect the Church, to fight against treachery, to protect the poor from injustice, to make peace in your own lands, to shed blood for your brethren [brothers], to lay down your own life.

Source B Christ leads a band of knights on a Crusade to capture the Holy Lands

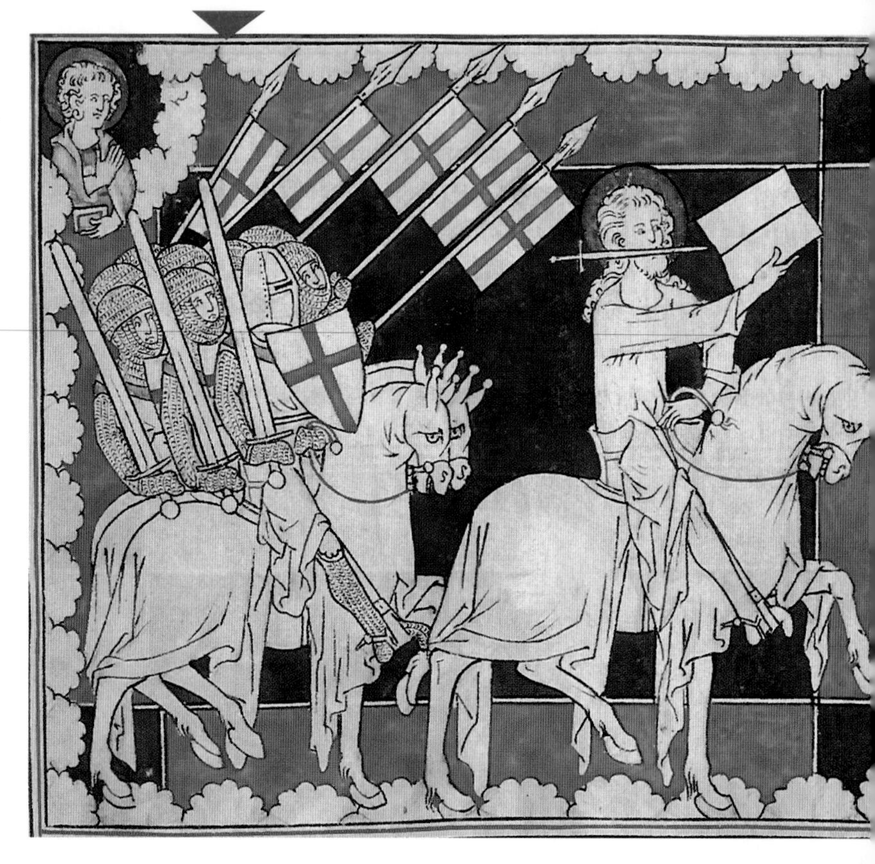

Source C Sir Geoffrey Luttrell sets out for a tournament. His wife and daughter-in-law wish him luck and hand him his helmet. From the Luttrell Psalter, made in 1342.

A steyght hed, a large brest, gret sholders, wel shapen arms – long and bygge, wel made long handes of grete bones, small bely, bygge thyes, leggis steyght.

Source D A description of a perfect knight. From *The Book of Fayttes of Armes*, a handbook of chivalry and warfare written by a woman, Christine de Pisan, in 1408–9.

Source E Sparing the enemy, by Oderic Vitalis, in about 1130

I have been told that in a battle in which about 900 knights fought, only three were killed. They were all clad in mail [*armour*] and spared each other on both sides because of their fear of God and their fellowship in arms. They were more concerned to capture prisoners than to kill them.

Source F By Peter of Blois, Archdeacon of Bath, in the foureenth century

The order of knighthood in these days of ours is mere disorder. For he who has the foulest mouth, who has the worst oaths, who least fears God and his priests – that man is said to be the bravest. When these knights go into battle they are laden not with steel but with wine.

Source G The horrors of war – a town is looted during the Hundred Years War

Source H The French nobility take their revenge against peasants who rebelled in 1358. A picture from an illustrated copy of Froissart's *Chronicle*, 1460.

Investigations

1 Look at Sources **A** and **B**. Why do you think the Church supported the idea of chivalry?

2 What evidence is there in Source **C** that Sir Geoffrey is dressed for show rather than going to war?

3 Source **D** is written in medieval English. Can you write it out in modern English? Can you think of any modern equivalents of this perfect knight?

4 What evidence is there in Source **E** that chivalry saved lives?

5 What examples of bad behaviour can you find in Sources **F** and **G**? Choose five of the examples and list them in order with the worst behaviour at the top. Explain why these sorts of behaviour are unchivalrous.

6 Compare Sources **E** and **H**. Why do you think the knights are behaving differently in each source?

Remember...

- **Chivalry was a system of rules to control the behaviour of knights.**
- **Chivalry was supported by the Church.**
- **Knights did not always behave in a chivalrous way.**

Tournaments

What happened at a tournament?

Tournaments were introduced into England from France by King Richard I 'the Lionheart' in the twelfth century. At first they were mock battles where young knights could prove their skills and courage. Although weapons were blunt, injuries and deaths were common. The Church tried to ban these bloody contests, but gradually came to approve of them as a way of training knights for the Crusades.

By the thirteenth century, tournaments were carefully managed by a 'marshal' who was ordered to arrange them by the king. They became a sporting and social event for the nobility. Combat was now usually between two 'champions' who charged at each other with long wooden lances. Barriers to prevent horses crashing into one another were not used until the fifteenth century.

Source A In 1390 French knights challenged English knights to a tournament at St Inglebert, near Calais – this account is from Froissart's *Chronicle*

Boucicaut v. the Earl of Huntingdon:

These two knights drew back from one another a certain space. When each of them had challenged the other they spurred their horses and charged violently. Boucicaut stuck the other through the shield and the lance head glanced over his arm and did him no harm. This round was well praised.

Source B A **melée**. Melées were held at dusk so that darkness would eventually stop the fighting if the knights got out of control.

Source C Lances shatter as two knights **joust**, and one falls

Key words

Melée A mock battle, involving many knights.
Joust A face-to-face challenge involving two knights with long lances.

Remember...

- **The first tournaments were mock battles, but later became a combat between two knights.**
- **Tournaments were a way of training knights.**

Investigations

1 Look at Source **B**.
a) What dangers can you see?
b) Why would a melée be good practice for war?
c) Can you suggest why it was difficult to control knights during a melée? Draw up a set of rules to make the melée safer.

2 Compare Sources **A** and **C**.
a) What are the dangers of jousting?
b) Why do you think jousting was believed to be more skilled than the melée?

Courtly love

What were the medieval rules for romance?

Rules of behaviour went beyond the battlefield to affect the personal lives of knights. Woman-hunting was a favourite sport. Courtly love was a romantic game in which a knight would try to win the heart of a lady. It did not matter if the lady was married or not, as the relationship was not meant to be too serious. Knights had to show their devotion by reciting poetry, playing music and doing great deeds. Courtly love was widely approved of because it civilised tough men of war. They had to behave well so as not to dishonour their ladies. They even had to keep clean!

Sometimes the game went too far, and couples had affairs. If the married ladies' husbands found out, they had two choices. They could ignore what was happening, perhaps because *they* were chasing other married women, or they had the right to kill their unfaithful wives and their lovers.

Source A A knight woos his lady. A picture in a thirteenth-century German manuscript.

Source B By Robert of Blois, a thirteenth-century French poet

> A woman should not look at a man as a sparrowhawk does a lark.

Source C A medieval story of courtly love briefly retold by the historian Barbara Tuchman in *A Distant Mirror*, 1980

> A knight falls madly in love with his lady. Her jealous husband lures him away into the Third Crusade. The knight fights well and fights gloriously but is eventually wounded by a poisoned arrow. He composes a last song and a farewell letter to be sent to his love after his death in a box – together with his **embalmed** heart. His faithful servant carries the box home but is caught by the husband. He has the heart cooked and served to his wife. On being told what she has eaten she swears that after such a noble food she will never eat again. She stands by her oath and dies of starvation. Her husband spends the rest of his life on **pilgrimages** hoping to be forgiven by God.

Key words

Embalmed Preserved.
Pilgrimage Travelling to holy places, like Jerusalem.

Remember...

- **Courtly love was a set of rules for controlling the way in which knights behaved towards women.**

Investigations

1. What is the knight doing in Source **A**? Why might a lady expect this?
2. What does the poet in Source **B** mean? How does this show that ladies encouraged the game of courtly love?

Protecting the past

What are we doing to protect medieval buildings?

Buildings from the Middle Ages are one of the most important parts of Britain's heritage. Cathedrals and churches built for the glory of God or castles raised for defence have stood the test of time. Often they became the core around which modern towns have grown.

Today they may be sources of local pride, helping communities by attracting thousands of tourists. However they are also a great responsibility, because they are very expensive to run and repair.

The city of Durham, dominated by its great Norman cathedral and castle, was declared a World Heritage Site by UNESCO (United Nations Educational, Scientific and Cultural Organisation) in 1987. Only a few places in Britain are thought special enough to deserve this title. Others include Stonehenge in Wiltshire and Ironbridge in Shropshire. The following sources look at the problems faced by Durham in protecting its medieval past.

Source A An aerial view of Durham – can you spot the castle and cathedral?

Source B Durham. From the *Guardian* newspaper, 26 June 1993.

The great Norman castle and cathedral are amongst the most majestic sites in Britain, the immense walls of rust brown stone rising sheer of the little streets and the wooded loop of the river which wraps right round the fortified centre of the tiny city.

But it's not for the view that Durham is listed as a World Heritage Site. Walk down from the station, and with every step the sense of history grows. Enter the old town, it's no great size, you could stroll across it in 20 minutes. Cobbled streets of old-fashioned shop fronts wind down to the market square. All around are attractive stone facades, Victorian and Georgian.

The Prince-Bishops of Durham were powerful nobles in the Middle Ages, minting their own coins and raising their own armies. County Durham is now advertised to tourists as 'The Land of the Prince-Bishops' (Source **C**).

Source C The symbol for the Land of the Prince-Bishops

Durham Castle today launches a £2.5 million appeal to prevent the collapse of its crumbling towers and walls. The defences of the castle have been weakened by almost a thousand years of weathering, worsened in recent decades by atmospheric pollution. A bucketful of debris a day is collected from the Norman entrance arch.
'A lot of the woodwork is alive with dry rot, wet rot, the whole lot,' said Albert Cartmell, the bursar. 'It looks solid but its like a pie – a hard, crusty rim but soft inside'.

Source D From the *Guardian* newspaper, 8 October 1991

Source E Visitor figures for Durham Cathedral

1990	390 546
1991	393 493
1992	364 646
1993	439 436
1994	333 735

It costs around £700 000 a year to look after the fabric of the cathedral. We employ 16 craftsmen, mainly stonemasons and joiners. The roof was replaced recently and cost £1million. This has to be done every 100 years.

Source F Mr Hindley, Durham Cathedral Accountant, 1996

Source G Repair work to the structure of Durham Cathedral

Investigations

1. Why do you think Durham was pleased to be called a World Heritage Site? Find out why Stonehenge and Ironbridge are famous.
2. Look at Source **A**. Why do you think this site was chosen for building Durham castle and cathedral? What problems might this give modern tourists?
3. Do you think Source **C** is a good advertising slogan? Can you think of any similar advertising campaign for another medieval site, using people from history?
4. Thinking about Sources **D** and **G** and what you have been taught in science, make a list of the ways in which the environment today is damaging historic monuments.
5. Compare Sources **B** and **E**. What are the attractions of Durham for tourists? What problems are they likely to cause?
6. Look at Source **F**. Entry to Durham Cathedral is free to tourists.
   a) Why do you think the Church today does not want to charge an entry fee to churches and cathedrals?
   b) What else could the cathedral management do to raise money?

7 A long and winding road

1066 William of Normandy conquers England

1095 The Crusades begin

The murder of Thomas Beckett

How did things change between 1066 and 1485?

Change and continuity

Even if you could sit still forever, some things would **change**. You would change by getting older, and your appearance would change. Things would change around you – sometimes quickly, sometimes slowly. But you would still be you and the chair would still be a chair. When things don't change very much we call this **continuity**.

Investigations

1 Tudor Timespeak
Here are some facts about different aspects of life in 1066.
a) Make a copy of the chart.
b) Complete the chart for 1485, by writing a sentence or two to say how things had changed or stayed the same. The 'Writing' box has been completed for you.

2 If it were possible for the Norman lord and lady to speak to their descendants in 1485, what might the Tudor lord and lady tell them about:
a) how life had changed over those four hundred years;
b) the things that had stayed the same?

1066
The Kingdom The king was King of England only.
Government The king did not have to take advice from anyone.
The Church In 1066 almost everyone went to church. There was only one Christian Church, the Catholic Church, led by the Pope.
Land and farming In 1066 nearly everyone earned their living by farming. No peasant was free. They had to work on the lord's land and could not leave the village.
Towns There were no towns of any size except London and York. They were controlled by the king or the local lord.
Castles and architecture Castles were large square stone structures.
Knowledge about the world Only Europe and the Holy Lands were known by Europeans. America had not yet been discovered.
Writing All books had to be hand-written.
Life and death Life was very hard. People would starve to death if there were bad harvests.

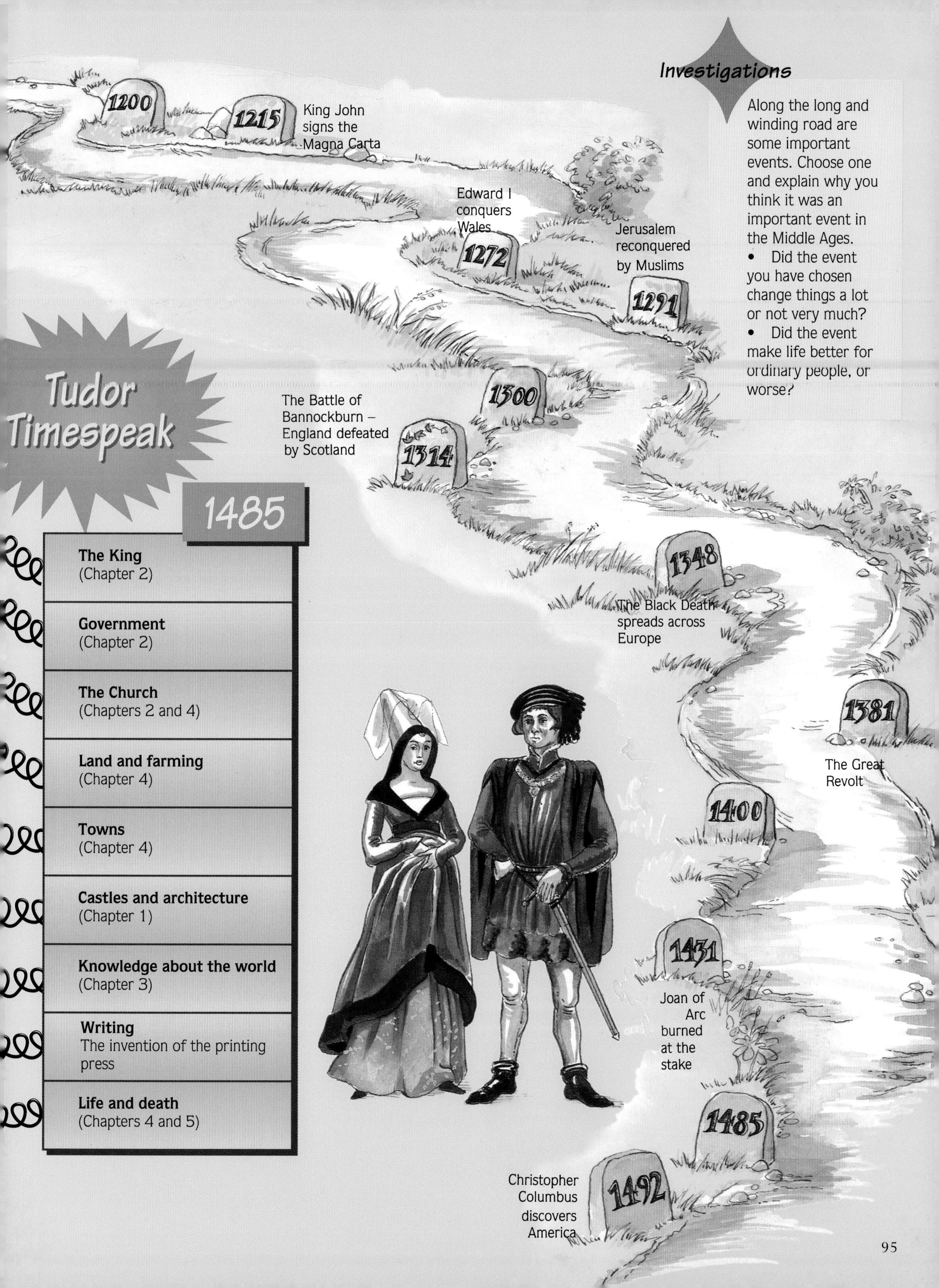

Tudor Timespeak

1485

The King (Chapter 2)
Government (Chapter 2)
The Church (Chapters 2 and 4)
Land and farming (Chapter 4)
Towns (Chapter 4)
Castles and architecture (Chapter 1)
Knowledge about the world (Chapter 3)
Writing The invention of the printing press
Life and death (Chapters 4 and 5)

Investigations

Along the long and winding road are some important events. Choose one and explain why you think it was an important event in the Middle Ages.

- Did the event you have chosen change things a lot or not very much?
- Did the event make life better for ordinary people, or worse?

Index